Robert Kleinschroth
Pete Oldham

Englisch an Stationen 5/6

SPEZIAL

Grammatik

listen

write

read

Die Herausgeber:

Marco Bettner: Rektor als Ausbildungsleiter, Haupt- und Realschullehrer, Referent in der Lehrerfort- und Lehrerweiterbildung

Dr. Erik Dinges: Rektor einer Förderschule für Lernhilfe, Referent in der Lehrerfort- und Lehrerweiterbildung

Die Autoren:

Robert Kleinschroth: Fachlehrer für Englisch und Französisch, erfahrener Autor von Englisch- und Französischlehrwerken

Pete Oldham: Fachlehrer für Englisch und Geschichte in England und Deutschland, erfahrener Autor von Englischlehrwerken

3. Auflage 2021
© 2013 Auer Verlag, Augsburg
AAP Lehrerwelt GmbH
Alle Rechte vorbehalten.

Das Werk als Ganzes sowie in seinen Teilen unterliegt dem deutschen Urheberrecht. Der*die Erwerber*in der Einzellizenz ist berechtigt, das Werk als Ganzes oder in seinen Teilen für den eigenen Gebrauch und den Einsatz im eigenen Präsenz- oder Distanzunterricht zu nutzen.
Produkte, die aufgrund ihres Bestimmungszweckes zur Vervielfältigung und Weitergabe zu Unterrichtszwecken gedacht sind (insbesondere Kopiervorlagen und Arbeitsblätter), dürfen zu Unterrichtszwecken vervielfältigt und weitergegeben werden.
Die Nutzung ist nur für den genannten Zweck gestattet, nicht jedoch für einen schulweiten Einsatz und Gebrauch, für die Weiterleitung an Dritte einschließlich weiterer Lehrkräfte, für die Veröffentlichung im Internet oder in (Schul-)Intranets oder einen weiteren kommerziellen Gebrauch.
Mit dem Kauf einer Schullizenz ist die Schule berechtigt, die Inhalte durch alle Lehrkräfte des Kollegiums der erwerbenden Schule sowie durch die Schüler*innen der Schule und deren Eltern zu nutzen.
Nicht erlaubt ist die Weiterleitung der Inhalte an Lehrkräfte, Schüler*innen, Eltern, andere Personen, soziale Netzwerke, Downloaddienste oder Ähnliches außerhalb der eigenen Schule.
Eine über den genannten Zweck hinausgehende Nutzung bedarf in jedem Fall der vorherigen schriftlichen Zustimmung des Verlags.

Sind Internetadressen in diesem Werk angegeben, wurden diese vom Verlag sorgfältig geprüft. Da wir auf die externen Seiten weder inhaltliche noch gestalterische Einflussmöglichkeiten haben, können wir nicht garantieren, dass die Inhalte zu einem späteren Zeitpunkt noch dieselben sind wie zum Zeitpunkt der Drucklegung. Der Auer Verlag übernimmt deshalb keine Gewähr für die Aktualität und den Inhalt dieser Internetseiten oder solcher, die mit ihnen verlinkt sind, und schließt jegliche Haftung aus.

Autor*innen: Robert Kleinschroth, Pete Oldham
Illustrationen: Steffi Aufmuth, Corina Beurenmeister, Julia Flasche, Stefanie Groß, Steffen Jähde, Ursula Lassert, Stefan Leuchtenberg, Stefan Lohr, Pete Oldham, Thorsten Trantow, Bettina Weyland, Georg Wieborg
Satz: Fotosatz H. Buck, Kumhausen
Druck und Bindung: Esser printSolutions GmbH, Bretten
CD-Pressung: optimal media production GmbH, Röbel/Müritz
ISBN 978-3-403-**07050**-4

www.auer-verlag.de

Inhaltsverzeichnis

Vorwort 5

Route Card 6

Basics
Station 1	Basic grammatical terms..	7
Station 2	Pronouns (1)	8
Station 3	Adjectives.............	9
Station 4	Adverbs (1)............	10
Station 5	Modal auxiliaries	11
Station 6	Prepositions...........	13
Station 7	Irregular plurals	14
Station 8	Simple present	15
Station 9	Questions and short answers	16
Station 10	Present progressive......	17
Station 11	Questions and question words	18

Mixed grammar
Station 1	Grammatical terms	19
Station 2	The present tense of *be* ..	20
Station 3	The simple past forms of *be*	21
Station 4	Present: simple or progressive? (1)	22
Station 5	Imperatives............	23
Station 6	Simple past (1)	24
Station 7	Simple past – irregular verbs	25
Station 8	Pronouns (2)	26
Station 9	Adverbs (2)............	27
Station 10	Adjectives and adverbs ...	28
Station 11	*Some/any*	29
Station 12	Simple past (2)..........	30

Tenses
Station 1	Past, present and future ..	32
Station 2	Present: simple or progressive? (2)	33
Station 3	Past progressive	34
Station 4	Past: simple or progressive?............	35
Station 5	Present perfect..........	36
Station 6	Present perfect with *for* and *since*	37
Station 7	Past and perfect.........	38
Station 8	Mixed tenses	39
Station 9	Past participles	40

Mixed bag
Station 1	Comparison of adjectives .	41
Station 2	Comparison of adverbs ...	42
Station 3	Present and future	43
Station 4	The *will*-future	44
Station 5	The *going to*-future	45
Station 6	Future with *going to* or *will*	46
Station 7	Conditional sentences, type 1	47
Station 8	Present perfect – word order	48
Station 9	A taste of phrasal verbs...	49
Station 10	A mixed bag of tenses	50

Solutions 51

Transcripts of the listening comprehension texts 63

Inhaltsverzeichnis CD

Basics

Track 1 (2:06 min)
Station 3: Adjectives, Tasks 1 and 2 (S. 9)

Track 2 (1:52 min)
Station 8: Simple present, Task 2 (S. 15)

Track 3 (1:22 min)
Station 10: Present progressive, Task (S. 17)

Mixed grammar

Track 4 (0:52 min)
Station 6: Simple past (1), Task 3 (S. 24)

Track 5 (1:25 min)
Station 7: Simple past – irregular verbs, Task 2 (S. 25)

Track 6 (0:55 min)
Station 10: Adjectives and adverbs, Tasks 1 and 2 (S. 28)

Tenses

Track 7 (1:10 min)
Station 4: Past: simple or progressive?, Tasks 1 and 2 (S. 35)

Mixed bag

Track 8 (3:01 min)
Station 1: Comparison of adjectives, Task (S. 41)

Track 9 (1:17 min)
Station 3: Present and future (Part 1), Task 1 (S. 43)

Track 10 (3:32 min)
Station 3: Present and future (Part 2), Task 2 (S. 43)

Track 11 (1:25 min)
Station 8: Present perfect – word order, Task 2 (S. 48)

Vorwort

Die Stationen und Materialien dieser Reihe bieten den Schülern[1] Arbeitsformen an, die ihr unterschiedliches Lerntempo und ihre unterschiedlichen Lernvoraussetzungen berücksichtigen. Allen Heften liegen die didaktischen Prinzipien der Schüler- und Handlungsorientiertheit, der Selbsttätigkeit und Nachhaltigkeit zugrunde. Sie basieren ferner auf der Lernpsychologie und kommen dem persönlichen Lerntyp der Schüler entgegen.

Schülerorientiertheit bedeutet, dass der Lehrer in den Hintergrund tritt. Anders als im lehrerzentrierten Unterricht wird ihm die Aufgabe des Aufbereitens und Vermittelns des Lernstoffs abgenommen. Er kann sich seiner pädagogischen Rolle des Beobachters, Beraters und Moderators widmen. Als Moderator hat er die Möglichkeit zur Binnendifferenzierung; er kann lernschwächere Schüler fördern und lernstärkere mit anspruchsvolleren Aufgaben fordern.

Handlungsorientiertheit und Selbsttätigkeit bedeuten, dass die Schüler das Wissen nicht aus zweiter Hand vom Lehrer übernehmen, sondern es sich selbstbestimmt und selbsttätig in der Auseinandersetzung mit den Lerngegenständen der Stationen erarbeiten. Sie wählen die Reihenfolge der Aufgaben, bestimmen das Arbeitstempo und, wo möglich, auch die Sozialformen wie Partner- oder Gruppenarbeit.

Die Arbeit an Stationen fördert das individuelle und nachhaltige Lernen. Viele Unterrichtsgegenstände, vor allem im Sachunterricht, werden den Grundlerntypen, den vorwiegend auditiv, visuell, kommunikativ und motorisch Lernenden gerecht. Dabei lernt der Schüler nicht nur über seinen dominanten Eingangskanal, sondern mit allen Sinnen, mit Auge, Ohr, Geruchs- und Tastsinn. Je mehr Sinne beim Lernen beteiligt sind, umso nachhaltiger wird das Wissen verankert. Dieses Wissen lässt sich umso leichter wieder abrufen, als es mit der Lernsituation und dem Lernort verknüpft wird (Loci-Lernen).

Das vorliegende Heft zur Grammatik der Klassen 5 und 6 deckt die Lehrpläne der Bundesländer ab. Es eignet sich sowohl für das Stationenlernen als auch für die Freiarbeit. Bei der Freiarbeit erhalten die Schüler einen Arbeitsplan, der innerhalb einer Frist zu erfüllen ist. Beim Stationenlernen liegen die Arbeitsblätter an Tischen aus. Sorgen Sie bitte, wo erforderlich, für ausreichend Wörterbücher, Abspielgeräte und Kopfhörer.

Der Grammatikstoff der Klassen 5 und 6 ist auf die Stationen der folgenden vier Gruppen verteilt:
- Basics
- Mixed grammar
- Tenses
- Mixed bag

---

[1] Aufgrund der besseren Lesbarkeit ist in diesem Buch mit Schüler auch immer Schülerin gemeint. Ebenso verhält es sich mit Lehrer und Lehrerin etc.

Route Card

for _____

Obligatory stations

Station number	done	checked
number _____		
number _____		
number _____		
number _____		
number _____		
number _____		
number _____		
number _____		
number _____		

Optional stations

Station number	done	checked
number _____		
number _____		
number _____		
number _____		
number _____		

Station 1

Basic grammatical terms

Name:

Task 1

Fill in an example of each grammatical term from the box below.

> the   cup   he   with
> hungry   his   must   a/an   and   badly   dance

	ENGLISH	GERMAN	EXAMPLE
1.	adjective	*Adjektiv*	_____
2.	adverb	*Adverb*	_____
3.	definite article	*bestimmter Artikel*	_____
4.	indefinite article	*unbestimmter Artikel*	_____
5.	conjunction	*Konjunktion*	_____
6.	personal pronoun	*Personalpronomen*	_____
7.	possessive pronoun	*Possessivpronomen*	_____
8.	infinitive form	*Infinitiv*	_____
9.	modal auxiliary	*modales Hilfsverb*	_____
10.	noun	*Nomen*	_____
11.	preposition	*Präposition*	_____

Task 2

Link the words in English (1–8) with the German translations (A–H).

1. (to) fill sth in   A) *beschreiben*
2. task   B) *etw mit etw verbinden*
3. (to) link sth with sth   C) *Übersetzung*
4. missing   D) *etw ausfüllen*
5. gap   E) *getan, ausgeführt*
6. done   F) *Aufgabe*
7. describe   G) *Lücke*
8. translation   H) *fehlend*

1 [ ]   2 [ ]   3 [ ]   4 [ ]   5 [ ]   6 [ ]   7 [ ]   8 [ ]

Station 2

Pronouns (1)

Name:

Pronomen sind Fürwörter. Sie stehen für (= *pro*) Hauptwörter (= *nomen*):
Tom likes **Tina** and **Tina** likes **Tom.** = **He** likes **her** and **she** likes **him.**
Tom and Tina like **their teachers.** = **They** like **them. We** like **our** teachers, too.

Task 1

Link the three types of pronouns. The first one is done for you.

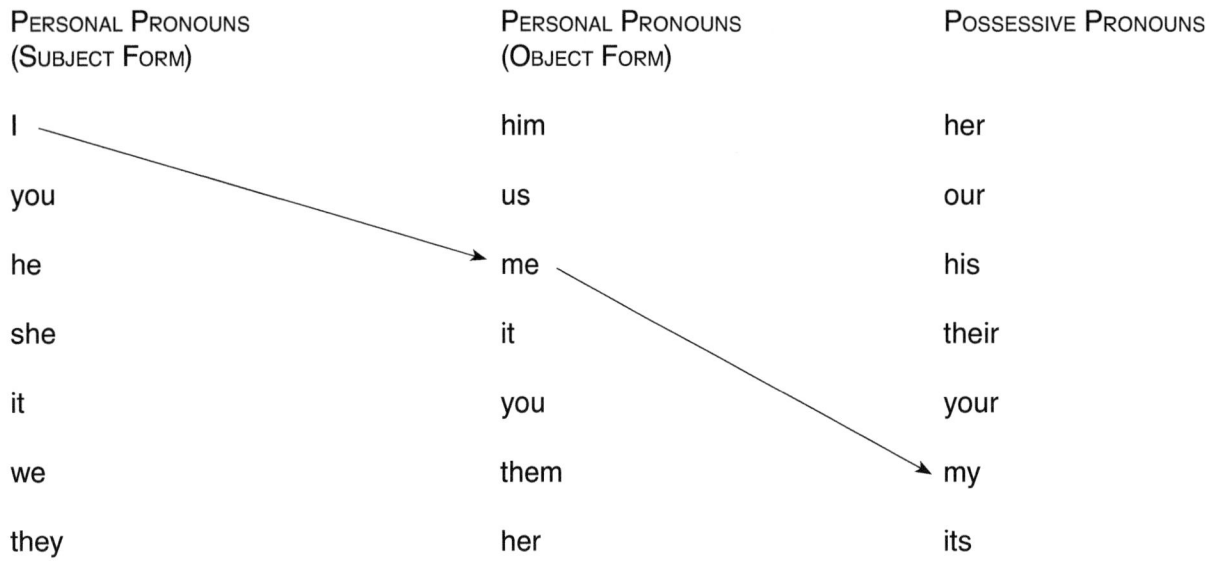

PERSONAL PRONOUNS (SUBJECT FORM)	PERSONAL PRONOUNS (OBJECT FORM)	POSSESSIVE PRONOUNS
I	him	her
you	us	our
he	me	his
she	it	their
it	you	your
we	them	my
they	her	its

Task 2

Fill in the missing pronouns from the box below.

> We   she   My   He   ~~my~~   they   us
> ~~I~~   them   him   them   they   her   me   she

_____I_____¹ like everybody in _____my_____² class and _____³ all like _____⁴, too. But Paul isn't so happy. _____⁵ likes Emily, a girl in another class, but _____⁶ doesn't like _____⁷. Paul sends _____⁸ notes, but Emily doesn't read _____⁹. _____¹⁰ family knows Emily's family because _____¹¹ live near _____¹². _____¹³ call Emily the Ice Queen because _____¹⁴ doesn't like other people and doesn't talk to _____¹⁵. Emily only likes cats and horses.

8

Station 3

Adjectives

Name:

Task 1 "Track 1"

Listen to Ian talk about a class visit to a chocolate factory. Then describe the pictures below by choosing an adjective from one box and a noun from the other.

fresh ~~friendly~~ useful crispy (knusprig) giant (riesig) white yellow interesting

boots (Stiefel) hat and coat croissants ~~guide~~ brochures mixer video film orange juice

1.
friendly guide

2.
_____

3.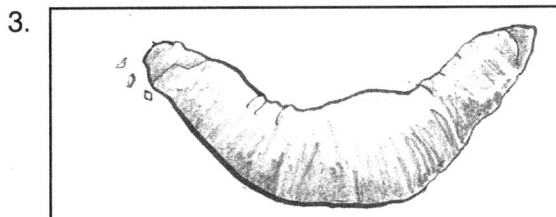
_____

4.
_____

5.
_____

6.
_____

7. _____

8. _____

Task 2 "Track 1"

Listen to Ian again. Use the pictures above to write a report about the class visit.

Station 4

Adverbs (1)

Name:

Basics

> Adjektive beschreiben Personen und Dinge: *I'm a **wonderful** singer*.
> Adverbien beschreiben hauptsächlich Verben: *I sing **wonderfully***.
> Die meisten Adverbien bildet man durch Anhängen von *-ly* an das Adjektiv: *soft – **softly**, happy – **happily***.
> Beachte: Adjectiv *good* – Adverb *well*.

Task 1

Read the following text. Highlight the adjectives and the adverbs in different colours. Use the information from the box above.

Mrs Corrigan has got two young daughters, Anne and Susan. They are the same size and they can wear each other's clothes easily. When they both want the same thing, they argue about it loudly. One day Anne and Susan have a very loud argument about a blouse. Their poor mother has a bad headache. After ten long minutes Mrs Corrigan loses her patience (*Geduld*) and acts quickly. She roughly pulls the blouse out of her daughters' hands and slowly tears it up (*zerreißen*) into small bits. "That's the end of the argument!" she shouts angrily. Then she looks carefully at the ruined blouse. It isn't one of her daughter's blouses. It's her new blouse!

Task 2

Translate these two sentences into German.

1. Uncle Harry smells bad. _____

2. Uncle Harry smells badly. _____

Task 3

The words in brackets are adverbs of frequency (*Häufigkeit*). Rewrite the sentence with the adverb in the correct place.

1. (often)   Dad reads the morning newspaper at breakfast.

   _____

2. (sometimes)   Mum asks him for the page with the crossword puzzle.

   _____

3. (usually)   I don't eat more than a slice (*Scheibe*) of toast for breakfast.

   _____

Station 5

Modal auxiliaries

Name: _____

Modale Hilfsverben haben nur eine Form für alle Personen:
*Peter **can swim**. I **can surf**. She **can sing**. They **can cook**.*
Frage und Kurzantwort: *Can he play the piano? – Yes, he can./No, he can't.*

Task 1

Highlight the modal auxiliaries. What are they in German?

1. Can I have another chocolate biscuit, please? _____
2. My dog can dance the tango. _____
3. When you are finished, you can leave. _____
4. Who will win the game? _____
5. May I open the window, please? _____
6. We must learn all these words by next Monday. _____
7. We needn't pay for these drinks – they're free! _____

Task 2

Complete the questions and short answers about Rex. Use modal auxiliaries.

1. _____ he dance the tango _____ ? – Yes, he _____ .
2. _____ he cook meals _____ ? – No, he _____ .
3. _____ ? – _____ .
4. _____ ? – _____ .
5. _____ ? – _____ .
6. _____ ? – _____ .

Rex:
✓ dance tango
✗ cook meals
✓ paint pictures
✗ catch cats
✓ eat anything
✗ do Maths homework

Task 3

Match the three phrases in the box (A, B, C) with the questions (1–6).

1. Can I use your red felt tip, please?
2. Can you swim 100 metres in fifty seconds?
3. Can you do some shopping for me?
4. Can you drive a tractor?
5. Can you help me with my Maths homework?
6. Can I go to the toilet, please?

A) *um einen Gefallen bitten*
B) *nach einer Fähigkeit fragen*
C) *um Erlaubnis bitten*

1 ☐   2 ☐   3 ☐   4 ☐   5 ☐   6 ☐

Station 5

Modal auxiliaries

Name:

| Beachte: | may (*dürfen*) | mustn't (*nicht dürfen*) |
| | must (*müssen*) | needn't (*nicht müssen, nicht brauchen*) |

Task 4

Match the English and the German expressions.

1. She can.
2. She can't.
3. She may.
4. She must.
5. She mustn't.
6. She needn't.
7. She will.
8. She won't.

A) Sie muss.
B) Sie wird nicht.
C) Sie braucht nicht.
D) Sie darf nicht.
E) Sie kann.
F) Sie darf.
G) Sie kann nicht.
H) Sie wird.

1  2 3  4  5 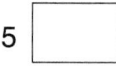 6  7 8

Task 5

Kevin isn't perfect. Complete the questions and the short answers.

1. _____n Kevin drive a car?   – No, he _____.
2. _____l he be a star?   – No, he _____.
3. _____t he learn English?   – Yes, he _____.

| Im *Simple present* kann **must** durch **have to** ersetzt werden. |
| **Must** you leave so soon? – Yes, my sister **must** cook a meal and I **must** help her. |
| **Do** you **have to** leave so soon? – Yes, my sister **has to** cook a meal and I **have to** help her. |

Task 6

Rewrite the following sentences with the correct form of *have to*.

1. You must sit here.
2. Why must we sit here?
3. Simon must try harder.
4. Simon must do his homework.
5. Must his Mum help him?

Station 6

Prepositions

Name:

Task 1

Complete the following sentences with a preposition of time or place *(on, at, in)*.

Invitation

My birthday is _____ [1] June. It's _____ [2] 16th June. I'm having a

birthday party _____ [3] Wendy's hamburger restaurant _____ [4]

Patterson Street. That's _____ [5] the new shopping arcade _____ [6]

the city centre. My party starts _____ [7] 5:30 _____ [8] the afternoon.

Please arrive _____ [9] time.

Alan

Task 2

Where is Romeo, the cat? Answer with one of the prepositions from the box.

| behind | in | under | in front of | on | between |

1.

He's _____ the sofa.

2.

He's _____ the books.

3.

He's _____ the TV.

4.

He's _____ his basket.

5.

He's _____ the chair.

6.

He's _____ the TV.

Station 7

Irregular plurals

Name:

Task 1

First translate these nouns into English. Then fill in the crossword with the English plural forms of these words.

Across

2. *Ehefrau* _____

4. *Messer* _____

5. *Person* _____

8. *Schaf* _____

9. *Zahn* _____

Down

1. *Mann* _____

2. *Frau* _____

3. *Kind* _____

6. *Pony* _____

7. *Fisch* _____

Task 2

Use a German-English dictionary and find the singular and plural forms of these words in English.

	Singular	Plural
1. *Wolf*	_____	_____
2. *Maus*	_____	_____
3. *Kopftuch*	_____	_____

Station 8

Simple present

Name: _____

Das *Simple present* wird verwendet
- für sich wiederholende Handlungen: *Tim often **plays** golf. He sometimes **plays** tennis.*
  Es steht oft mit Signalwörtern wie *sometimes, usually, always, never* usw.
- für aufeinander folgende Handlungen: *Tom **wakes up**, **gets up** and **dresses**.*

Task 1

Fill in the gaps with words from the box below. Use the correct form of the verbs.

> bark   call   not wear   put   not speak   try   walk   jump (2x)
> go   sit   brush   have (2x)   follow   lock   ~~ring~~   say   get

The alarm clock _____rings_____¹. I _____² up and _____³ Rex, my dog. A big, red cat _____⁴ out of my bed and _____⁵, "Hello, Tom." Very strange! Cats _____ usually _____⁶ English.

I _____⁷ to the bathroom. The big cat _____⁸ me. I always _____⁹ a shower and _____¹⁰ my teeth first thing in the morning. But the door is locked. So I _____¹¹ on my shirt and my socks. Very strange – they are much too big.

The big, red cat _____¹² onto the chair and _____¹³ down on my jeans. It _____¹⁴ just like Rex, "Wuff, wuff, wuff". Then it _____¹⁵ to get into my jeans. Very strange! Cats _____ usually _____¹⁶ jeans.

I go downstairs to the kitchen – the cat _____¹⁷ in front of me. We often _____¹⁸ breakfast in the kitchen. But the door is locked. Mum never _____¹⁹ the kitchen door. Very strange …

Task 2 "Track 2"

Now listen to the story and check your answers. Then write an ending to the story on the other side of the worksheet.

Task 3

Highlight the signal words for simple present in Task 1.

15

Station 9

Questions and short answers

Name:

Basics

Beantworte Entscheidungsfragen nicht nur mit *Yes* oder *No*. Sei höflich und sage: *Yes, I do./No, I don't./Yes, I have./No, I haven't./Yes, they are./No, they aren't.*
Does Rex like cats? – Yes, he **does**.   **Do** cats like Rex? – No, they **don't**.
Have you got a bike? – Yes, **I have**.   **Have** you got a car? – No, **I haven't**.

Task 1

It's a quiz. Tom tries to find out what Tina's pet is. Complete Tina's answers.

Tom:

1. Is your new pet big?
2. Does it bark?
3. Does it sing?
4. Does it catch mice?
5. Has it got legs?
6. Do you feed it every day?
7. I give up. Tell me, what is it?

   Ah, a _____.

Tina:

No, _____.

No, _____.

No, _____.

No, _____.

No, _____.

Yes, _____.

Here's a clue (*Hinweis*): It's a *shidflog*.

Yes, _____.

Task 2 *(Partnerarbeit)*

Now think of a pet and act out a dialogue quiz with your partner. Then change roles.

Task 3 *(Partnerarbeit)*

A new boy in your school. Complete Tom's questions and Tina's answers.

Tom:

1. _____ he a new boy?
2. _____ know his name?
3. _____ parents from Italy?
4. _____ they from Spain?
5. _____ got a pet?
6. _____ like him?
7. _____ his girlfriend?

Tina:

Yes, _____.

No, _____.

No, _____.

Yes, _____.

Yes, _____.

Yes, _____.

No, _____.

Station 10

Present progressive

Name: _____

Das *Present progressive* wird verwendet, wenn etwas gerade geschieht:
*I **am taking** photos. Tom **is reading**. We **are doing** our homework.*

Task "Track 3"

Listen carefully and then write a sentence about each picture. The words in the boxes below can help you. Use the correct present progressive forms of the verbs.

| chase *(jagen)* drive feed hold | birds from a bottle cow eggs |
| look for milk *(melken)* ride | ponies kitten *(Kätzchen)* tractor |

1. My name is Ellen.

   I _____.

2. Ellen:

   I _____.

3. Jane Cox works on the farm.

   She _____.

4. Tim and his sister Sally are in this photo.

   They _____.

5. This is a photo of Bob, the farmer's son.

   He _____.

6. These are Lisa and Anna from Germany.

   They _____.

7. They have got a big black dog. His name is Pinkie.

   He _____.

Station 11

Questions and question words

Name:

Task 1

Complete the interview with Hagrid. Use the right question words from the box.

Who   How   Why   Where   What   When   Whose

1. _____ are you today, Hagrid? – I'm fine, thank you.
2. _____ dog is this? – He's my dog. He isn't dangerous.
3. _____ 's your dog's name? – It's Fluffy.
4. _____ are all the boys and girls? – They are with their families.
5. _____ aren't they at school? – Because they are on holiday.
6. _____ do they come back to Hogwarts? – In September.
7. _____ is headmaster at Hogwarts? – It's Albus Dumbledore.

Task 2

Match the question words (A–I) with the rest of the questions (1–9). Write the numbers in the magic squares (*Quadrate*). If your answers are correct, all columns (*Spalten*) and rows (*Zeilen*) will add up to the magic number 15. Use a pencil and a rubber.

A) Who
B) Where
C) What
D) Whose
E) Which
F) How do
G) Why
H) Who do
I) When does

A _____	B _____	C _____
D _____	E _____	F _____
G _____	H _____	I _____

1. … Harry and Ron go to Hogwarts?
2. … is Harry's best friend? Draco?
3. … you like better? Draco or Ron?
4. … mustn't Harry use magic at home?
5. … of the pets is Ron's? The rat?
6. … colour is Harry's pet?
7. … is Hogwarts? Is it in Scotland?
8. … Harry stay at the Dursleys?
9. … pet is Fluffy?

Task 3

Translate these sentences. They all use the same question word.

1. *Wer hilft Hagrid?* _____
2. *Wem hilft Hagrid?* _____
3. *Wen mögen alle Schüler?* _____

Station 1

Grammatical terms

Name:

Task 1

Link the grammatical terms (1–10) with the examples (A–J).

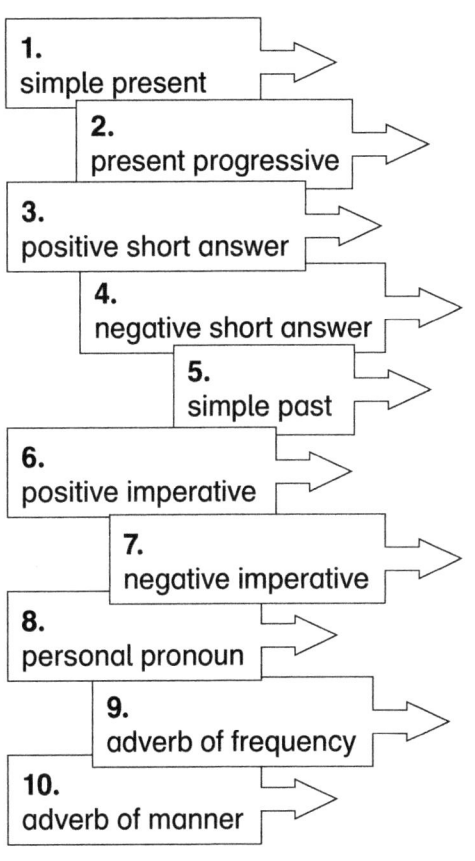
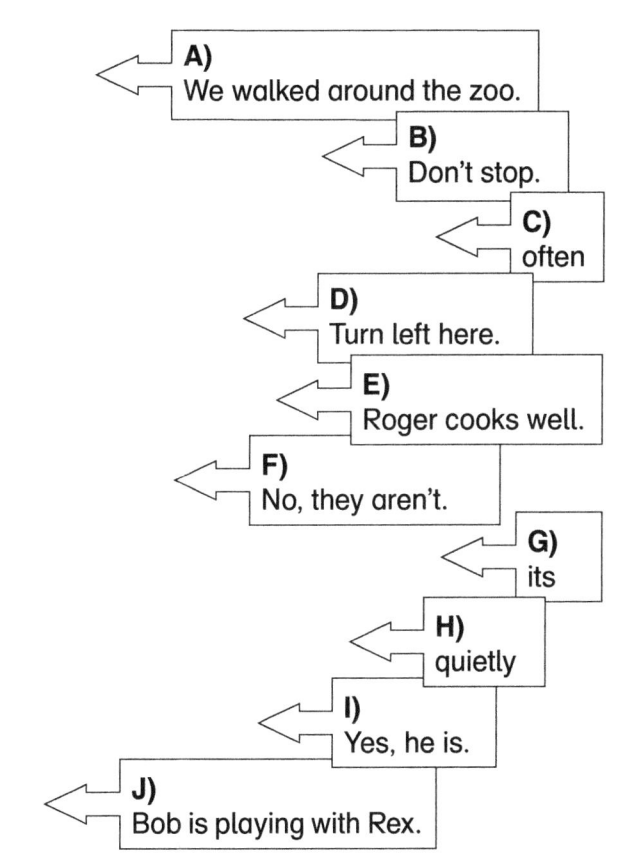

1. simple present
2. present progressive
3. positive short answer
4. negative short answer
5. simple past
6. positive imperative
7. negative imperative
8. personal pronoun
9. adverb of frequency
10. adverb of manner

A) We walked around the zoo.
B) Don't stop.
C) often
D) Turn left here.
E) Roger cooks well.
F) No, they aren't.
G) its
H) quietly
I) Yes, he is.
J) Bob is playing with Rex.

Mixed grammar

Task 2

Link the words in English (1–8) with the German translations (A–H).

1. practice
2. (to) practise
3. brackets
4. table
5. (to) complete
6. tense
7. (to) highlight
8. choose

A) *Klammern*
B) *(aus)wählen*
C) *Zeit*
D) *Übung*
E) *hervorheben*
F) *Tabelle*
G) *üben*
H) *vervollständigen*

1   2   3   4   5   6   7   8

Station 2

The present tense of be

Name:

In der Gegenwart hat *be* drei Formen: *am*, *is* und *are*.
In Fragen gehen die Verbformen dem Subjekt voraus: ***Are*** *you Sita?* ***Is*** *he your brother?* ***Am*** *I OK?*
Für **bejahte** Kurzantworten nimmst du die Langformen: *Yes, I am. / Yes, he is. / Yes, they are.*
Für **verneinte** Kurzantworten nimm die Kurzformen: *No, I'm not. / No, he isn't. / No, they aren't.*

Task 1

You're Ben. You're in the schoolyard with some friends. Mr Odd, your teacher, is old. He can't hear very well and has got a bad memory (*Gedächtnis*). Answer his questions.

Mr Odd:	**Ben:**
1. You must be the new boy. How are you?	_____ fine, thank you.
2. Is Lisa your sister?	No, _____.
3. You must be twins (*Zwillinge*), Lisa and you.	No, _____. We're friends.
4. But you're both at our school.	Yes, _____.
5. And you're both in class six.	No, _____. We're in class five.
6. Never mind (*Das macht nichts*), Sanjay.	But _____ Sanjay. I'm Ben!

Task 2

Complete the table with forms of *be*.

Question	Positive Answer	Negative Answer
1. _____ I your partner?	Yes, you _____.	No, you _____.
2. _____ Sanjay your brother?	Yes, _____.	No, _____.
3. _____ you twins?	Yes, _____.	No, _____.
4. _____ your parents from India?	Yes, _____.	No, _____.
5. _____ this Mr Odd's dog?	Yes, _____.	No, _____.
6. _____ you ready?	Yes, _____.	No, _____.

Task 3

Interview your partners. Write down your questions before the interview. Ask them if 1. they're new in your class; 2. they're English/Turkish/…; 3. their parents/grandparents are from India/Germany/…; 4. their brother/sister is at your school; 5. their brother/sister is older or younger; 6. they are good at Maths/English/…

Mixed grammar

Station 3

The simple past forms of be

Name: _____

> *Be* hat nur zwei *Simple past*-Formen: **was** und **were**. In Fragen gehen diese Formen dem Subjekt voraus: **Was** Bob at the party?/ **Were** Tom and Ellen at the party?
> Für **bejahte** Kurzantworten nimm die Langform: *Yes, he was./Yes, they were.*
> In der **verneinten** Kurzantwort steht die Kurzform: *No, he wasn't./No, they weren't.*

Task 1 *(Partnerarbeit)*

Complete the dialogue about a Halloween party. Use the simple past forms of *be*.
Then practise the dialogue with a 'Yes-girl' and a 'No-boy' from your class.

Ben's questions:	Lisa, the Yes-girl:	Bill, the No-boy:
1. _____ you at Sita's party, Lisa?	Yes, I _____.	No, you _____.
2. _____ Bob and Ron there, too?	Yes, they _____.	No, they _____.
3. _____ my costume super?	Yes, it _____.	No, it _____.
4. _____ the twins there?	Yes, they _____.	No, they _____.
5. _____ I the star of the party?	Yes, you _____.	No, you _____.
6. _____ Sita's parents nice?	Yes, they _____.	No, they _____.

Task 2

Ben and Ron are at the bank. Two masked robbers (*maskierte Räuber*) enter the bank. They take all the money and run away. An inspector questions the boys. Complete the interview. Be careful with the tense in the last question.
Then practice the interview with two classmates.

Inspector:	Ben:	Ron:
1. _____ you both at the bank?	Yes, we _____.	No, we _____.
2. _____ both men masked?	No, they _____.	Yes, they _____.
3. _____ the tall man armed (*bewaffnet*)?	Yes, he _____.	No, he _____.
4. _____ there a woman with them?	No, there _____.	Yes, there _____.
5. _____ you both short-sighted (*kurzsichtig*)?	Yes, we _____.	No, I _____, but Ben _____.

Mixed grammar

Station 4: Present: simple or progressive? (1)

Verwende das *Simple present*
- für Handlungen, die sich wiederholen (Signalwörter: *always, often, never*): *I always **get up** at 7 o'clock.*
- für Handlungen, die aufeinander folgen: *I **wash** and **put on** my clothes.*

Verwende das *Present progressive*, wenn etwas gerade geschieht (*now, just, today, at the moment*): *Tom **is having** breakfast right now.*

Task 1

Fill in the correct forms of the verbs in brackets.

1.

   Look! Mr Dobbs _____ (go) for a walk.

   He always _____ (walk) Rex at seven.

2.

   Every morning Rex _____ (run) to the kiosk,

   _____ (buy) a newspaper for Mr Dobbs

   and _____ (carry) it home in his mouth.

3.

   Here, Rex _____ (practise) skateboarding.

   Sometimes he _____ (go) to the kiosk by

   skateboard and _____ (buy) the paper.

4.
   It's ten o'clock. Mr Dobbs _____ (still sleep).

   So Rex _____ (read) the paper first.

   But he _____ (not do) this every day.

   On Sundays, he _____ (read) a book.

Task 2

Highlight the correct forms of the verbs.

Mr Dobb's friend Bill from Texas (1) *stays / is staying* in London for some days. He often (2) *comes / is coming* to see him. Today they (3) *visit / are visiting* London Zoo. They (4) *walk / are walking* over to the lions first and Bill says, "We (5) *have / are having* much bigger lions in Texas." In front of the kangaroo house they (6) *stop / are stopping* and Bill (7) *says / is saying*, "Wow! But your grasshoppers (*Grashüpfer*) are really much bigger than ours in Texas."

Station 5

Imperatives

Der bejahte Imperativ:	**Open** the door, please.
Der verneinte Imperativ:	**Don't shout**, please.
Der „Wir-Imperativ":	**Let's** go. (Gehen wir!)

Task

The Manners are in Italy on a holiday. Here are some signs they see on the way to their camping site. Complete the imperatives with words from the box.

> smoke   let's (2x)   take   leave   wear   turn (3x)
> keep   put   think   picnic   show

1. Careful! You can't go straight on. _____ right here.

2. _____ here, John. You must go straight on.

3. Oh Dad! This is a petrol station. _____ here.

4. Sorry, my boy. Please _____ your dog outside.

5. Nice place! But the sign says "_____ here."

6. Don't you see the sign? _____ the fire out at once.

7. Ben, no fishing. _____ your rod (Angelrute) back to the car.

8. No camping. _____ put the tent back into the car.

9. Ben, please _____ Rex on the leash (Leine) in the park.

10. No, Lisa. _____ your bikini in the museum.

11. Isn't that a nice place? – Yes, _____ stay here.

12. Please, _____ the music down, Ben.

   We're on a camping site. _____ of the neighbours.

13. Here's a policeman, Dad. _____ him the passports.

Station 6

Simple past (1)

Name: _____

Task 1

What do you know about the simple past? Tick off (✓) the correct answer.

1. The simple past of *call* is *called*. You take the infinitive and add *-ed*.
2. We use the simple past to speak of today, this week or tomorrow.
3. We use the simple past to talk about yesterday, last Tuesday, last year.
4. *Rex was catching mice at one o'clock* is an example of the simple past.

right	wrong

Task 2

Write the simple past form of the verbs in the box in the right group.

> copy, happen, hurry, jump, plan, tidy, spot, swap, trip, open, play, worry

GROUP 1
clos**ed**

_____
_____
_____
_____

GROUP 2
sto**pp**ed

_____
_____
_____
_____

GROUP 3
tr**i**ed

_____
_____
_____
_____

Task 3 "Track 4"

A surprise *(Überraschung)* for Mr Dobbs. Listen to the story of Mr Dobbs and the mousetrap *(Mausefalle)* and complete the table with the irregular verb forms from the story.

INFINITIVE   SIMPLE PAST

1. go   Mr Dobbs _____ to town.
2. buy   He _____ a mousetrap.
3. come   He _____ home.
4. see   He _____ no cheese.
5. think   He _____ very hard.
6. have   He _____ an idea.
7. draw   He _____ a picture.

Station 7

Simple past – irregular verbs

Name:

Task 1

Complete the table with the correct verb forms.

	German Infinitive	Simple Present	Simple Past
1.	gehen	I _____	I _____
2.	tun	he _____	he _____
3.	reiten	she _____	she _____
4.	finden	you _____	you _____
5.	werfen	we _____	we _____
6.	unterrichten	Jo _____	Jo _____
7.	stehlen	they _____	they _____
8.	sprechen	she _____	she _____
9.	sagen	he _____	he _____
10.	verlassen	you _____	you _____
11.	sehen	Bob _____	Bob _____

Task 2 "Track 5"

An interview with Wild Bill Hickock. Listen to the story. Then complete Bill's answers.

Reporter from the Deadwood Post:

1. Did you walk into Deadwood?
2. Did you go into the hotel?
3. Where did you leave your horse?
4. What did you say to the guests?
5. Was your horse still where you left it?
6. Did you report the theft (*den Diebstahl melden*) to the sheriff?
7. What did you do with your guns?
8. Did the guns fall onto your head?
9. And did you find the horse at last?
10. Tell me, what did you do in Texas?

Wild Bill Hickock:

1. No, I _____ into Deadwood.
2. No, I _____ into the bar.
3. I _____ it outside the bar.
4. I said, "Who _____ my horse?"
5. No, it _____.
6. No, I _____ back into the bar.
7. I _____ them into the air.
8. No, I _____ them.
9. Yes, I _____ it outside the bar.
10. Nothing. I _____ to walk home.

Mixed grammar

25

Station 8

Pronouns (2)

Name:

Task 1

Link the different types of pronouns (1–4) with the examples (A–D).

1. personal pronouns (subject form)

2. personal pronouns (object form)

3. possessive pronouns (subject form)

4. possessive pronouns (object form)

A)
my
your
his
her
its

our
your
their

B)
mine
yours
his
hers
–

ours
yours
theirs

C)
I
you
he
she
it

we
you
they

D)
me
you
him
her
it

us
you
them

1 [　]   2 [　]   3 [　]   4 [　]

Task 2

Use a marker pen and highlight the correct pronouns.

1. Does that pen belong to *my/me*? Yes, it's *mine/my*.

2. Ian, do *you/your* know the Gordons? What's *they/their* address?

3. Tell *they/them* that *we/us* can do the job.

4. We gave them *our/ours* telephone number and they gave us *their/theirs*.

5. Where is George? When did you last see *his/him*?

6. *It/Its* could belong to Diana. Yes, I'm sure *it/its* is *her/hers*.

7. *Me/I* can't find *mine/my* favourite CD. Have *you/yours* got *its/it*?

Station 9

Adverbs (2)

Name:

Task 1

Link the ships to the correct docks.

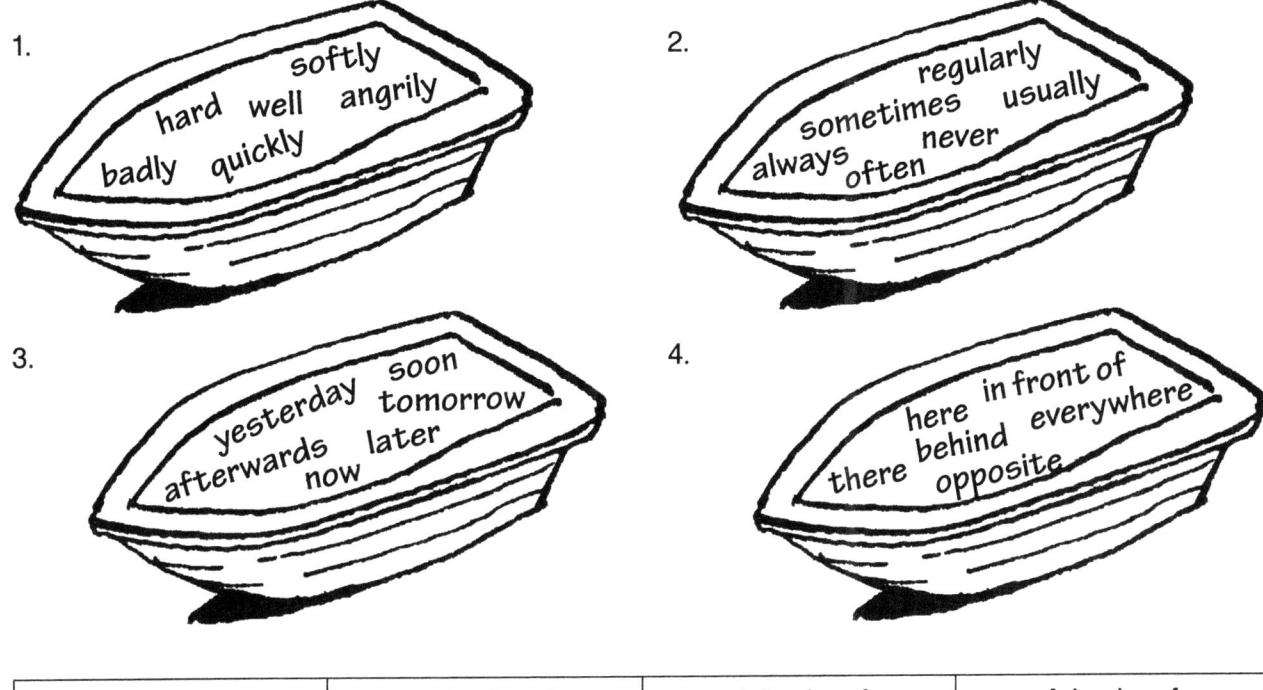

1. hard, well, softly, angrily, badly, quickly
2. regularly, sometimes, usually, always, often, never
3. yesterday, soon, tomorrow, afterwards, later, now
4. here, in front of, behind, everywhere, there, opposite

Adverbs of TIME	Adverbs of FREQUENCY (Häufigkeit)	Adverbs of MANNER (Art und Weise)	Adverbs of PLACE

Task 2

Highlight the adverbs that you don't know and look them up in an English-German dictionary.

Task 3

Fill in the gaps with a suitable adverb from Task 1.

1. The feather (*Feder*) landed _____, the stone landed _____.

2. The weather is fine today. _____ it rained all day.

3. I like this place and I come _____ often.

4. My cat often jumps _____ the TV when it wants attention (*Aufmerksamkeit*).

5. I hate rice pudding and I _____ eat it.

6. Tom cut himself _____ and his parents took him to hospital.

7. Poor Tom is in hospital. I hope he gets _____ _____.

8. I'm very busy _____, but I can meet you _____.

Station 10

Adjectives and adverbs

Name:

Task 1 "Track 6"

Listen to the story. Then listen again and fill in the gaps.

A police car stops _____¹ the bank and the police chief jumps _____². "Officer Doyle and I watched all the exits (*Ausgänge*)," a police officer tells her _____³, "and nobody left."

The police chief and the two police officers run _____⁴ into the bank. They search _____⁵, but they can't find the bank robber _____⁶. The police chief is _____⁷.

"How could the robber escape when you were watching every exit?" she asks the two police officers _____⁸.

"Well, ma'am," one of the police officers says _____⁹, "he was very _____¹⁰ and left by the entrance (*Eingang*)."

Task 2 "Track 6"

Listen to the story again and check your results. Highlight the adjectives and the adverbs in the story in different colours.

Task 3

Rewrite the sentences with the adjective and adverbs in brackets. Be careful with the word order.

1. (carefully) You must carry a bottle of TNT.

   _____

2. (yesterday) I went to a rock concert in the park.

   _____

3. (usually) I don't wear green socks with blue shoes.

   _____

4. (straight) The ball rolled across the road.

   _____

Station 11

Some/any

Name:

> Verwende **some** für
> - positive Aussagen: *There are some sandwiches on the table.*
> - Angebote: *Would you like some tea?*
> - höfliche Bitten: *Can I have some sugar, please?*
>
> Verwende **any** für
> - negative Aussagen: *We haven't got any money.*
> - allgemeine Fragen: *Do you have any pets?*
> - nach den Adverbien *never, without, hardly*: *I did it without any help.*

Task 1

Read the grammar box and then complete the following sentences with *some* or *any*.

1. I hope that there aren't _____ difficult questions in the test.
2. There are never _____ buses when you need one!
3. Alice, can you give me _____ help in the garden, please?
4. Have you got _____ relatives (*Verwandte*) who live in Australia?
5. Are there _____ biscuits left?
6. Would you like _____ milk in your tea?
7. I can see _____ cars in front of Mary's house.
8. _____ wild animals are dangerous (*gefährlich*).

Task 2

Complete the sentences with the correct compound of *some* or *any* (e. g. *something, anybody* etc.).

1. I can't find my socks. But they must be _____!
2. Where's Ann? I can't find her _____.
3. The house is empty. There isn't _____ there.
4. Trains are boring! There's hardly (*kaum*) _____ to do!
5. I'm hungry. Is there _____ in the fridge (*Kühlschrank*) to eat?
6. Yesterday _____ took my bike.
7. There's _____ in this box, but I don't know what it is.

Station 12

Simple past (2)

Name:

Diese Station besteht aus zwei Arbeitsblättern. Die Lösungen der ersten beiden Aufgaben helfen dir bei der dritten.

Task 1

Two German translations are correct, one translation is wrong. Highlight the two correct translations.

1. firm — *Firmung* — *fest* — *Firma*
2. to spend — *(Zeit) verbringen* — *spenden* — *(Geld) ausgeben*
3. to spy — *spicken* — *spionieren* — *ausspähen*
4. whisper — *wispern* — *wischen* — *flüstern*
5. surprise — *Erstaunen* — *Überraschung* — *saure Prise*
6. doorstep — *Torschuss* — *Türstufe* — *Türschwelle*
7. famous — *berühmt* — *berüchtigt* — *weltbekannt*

Task 2

Complete the table. Use the list of irregular verbs in your English book or a dictionary.

German Infinitive	Simple Present	Simple Past
1. *(Auto) fahren*	I _____	I _____
2. *finden*	he _____	he _____
3. *hören*	she _____	she _____
4. *halten*	you _____	you _____
5. *(be)halten*	we _____	we _____
6. *wissen*	Jo _____	Jo _____
7. *machen*	they _____	they _____
8. *sagen*	she _____	she _____
9. *sehen*	he _____	he _____
10. *verbringen*	Lina _____	Lina _____
11. *(aus)spionieren*	Bob _____	Bob _____
12. *denken*	I _____	I _____
13. *aufwachen*	he _____	he _____

Mixed grammar

Station 12

Simple past (2)

Name: _____

Task 3

Complete the text with the simple past forms of the verbs in brackets.

How Harry Potter came to live with the Dursleys

The Dursleys (be) _____¹ a perfectly normal family. Mr Dursley (be) _____² a director. His firm (make) _____³ drills (*Bohrer*). They (have) _____⁴ a fat son called Dudley and they (tell) _____⁵ everybody that he was the finest boy in the world.

Mrs Dursley (not work) _____⁶. She (spend) _____⁷ much of her time in the garden and (spy) _____⁸ on the neighbours. Nobody (know) _____⁹ that the Dursleys (have) _____¹⁰ a nephew (*Neffe*) called Harry and they (keep) _____¹¹ it secret (*geheim halten*).

Mr Dursley (wake) _____¹² up on a rainy Tuesday. On his way to work, he (see) _____¹³ funny people in funny clothes in the street and he (hear) _____¹⁴ them whisper something like Hurry Putter or Hurry Pitter. When he (drive) _____¹⁵ home in the evening, he no longer (think) _____¹⁶ about it.

The next morning, to their great surprise, Mr and Mrs Dursley (find) _____¹⁷ a baby on their doorstep. The baby (not wake up) _____¹⁸ but (sleep) _____¹⁹ on. One small hand (hold) _____²⁰ a letter for the Dursleys. The baby (not know) that _____²¹ he (be) _____²² special and famous and that it (be) _____²³ his job to save (*retten*) the world one day.

Station 1

Past, present and future

Name:

Task 1

Sort the following sentences into the three categories below.

1. ~~I like most ice cream, but not vanilla.~~
2. Yes, I was in town yesterday.
3. Your train leaves in two hours.
4. What are you playing?
5. Look. The Smiths have bought a new car.
6. Don't sit on the wet grass!
7. What did you watch?
8. Do you often visit your grandparents?
9. Please call me as soon as you arrive.
10. We're going to San Francisco next month.
11. I'm going to go for a walk after lunch.
12. No, we aren't going shopping, we're going for a walk.
13. Where were Alan and Joan?
14. We're playing a team from France next week.
15. When do you play snooker (*Billard*)?
16. I didn't play well.
17. I'll send you some photos with my next e-mail.
18. We were shopping in the market.

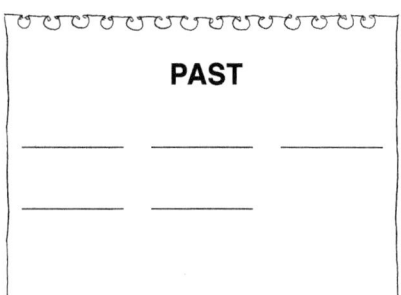

PAST

PRESENT (+ PERFECT)

1

FUTURE

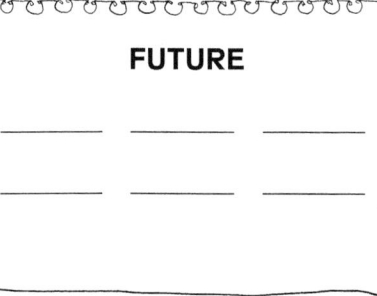

Task 2

Link the words in English (1–8) with the German translations (A–H).

1. comparative form   A) *Erklärung*
2. note   B) *nachschlagen*
3. describe   C) *Klammern*
4. look up   D) *Partizip*
5. explanation   E) *beschreiben*
6. brackets   F) *Notiz*
7. rhyming pairs   G) *Vergleichsform*
8. participle   H) *Reimpaare*

1 ☐   2 ☐   3 ☐   4 ☐   5 ☐   6 ☐   7 ☐   8 ☐

Station 2: Present: simple or progressive? (2)

Name:

> Verwende das *Simple present* für Handlungen, die man **regelmäßig** tut: *I always **do** my homework*.
> Verwende das *Present progressive* für Handlungen, die man **gerade** tut: *I'm **doing** my homework now*.

Task

Write sentences about Merlin's activities. Use the simple present and the present progressive. The first one is done for you.

This is what Merlin the magician *(Zauberer)* usually does:

9 a.m.	get up
10 a.m.	make breakfast
11 a.m.	fly around on his broom *(Besen)*
1 p.m.	cook lunch
2 p.m.	read magic books
3 p.m.	do magic
4 p.m.	teach magic at school
5 p.m.	dance with witches *(Hexen)*
6 p.m.	read a horror story
7 p.m.	clean his broom

Today is different. This is what Merlin is doing today:

9 a.m.	lie in bed and read
10 a.m.	have breakfast at the pub
11 a.m.	write letter to Harry Potter
1 p.m.	eat at Witches Club
2 p.m.	create magic flowers
3 p.m.	take dragon *(Drache)* Bert for a walk
4 p.m.	Bert and Merlin play tennis
5 p.m.	prepare a party
6 p.m.	create flying bikes
7 p.m.	Bert and Merlin ride their bikes

1. <u>Merlin usually gets up at 9 a.m., but today he's lying in bed and reading.</u>
2. _____
3. _____
4. _____
5. _____
6. _____
7. _____
8. _____
9. _____
10. _____

Station 3

Past progressive

Name: _____

> Das *Past progressive* wird mit **was** oder **were** und der **-ing-Form** des Verbs gebildet:
> Tom **was reading.** / **Were** they **reading?** – He **wasn't running.** / They **weren't crying**.

Task 1

Sheriff Wyatt asks the people in the bar what they were doing yesterday at nine o'clock when somebody stole Jack's horse. Complete his notes. Use the past progressive.

1. play poker

2. polish his saddle

3. clean his revolvers

4. drink beer

5. play the piano

6. wait outside

1. John and Jim were _____.

2. Frank _____.

3. Mac says he _____.

4. Ron and Harry say, "_____."

5. The cowboy _____.

6. The horse says, "_____."

Task 2

Simple or progressive? Highlight the correct verb forms.

> A plane (1) *circled / was circling* at ten thousand metres and the new parachutists (*Fallschirmspringer*) (2) *got ready / were getting ready* for their first jump. "Stop!" (3) *shouted / was shouting* the captain, "You (4) *weren't wearing / aren't wearing* your parachutes."
>
> "It's okay, captain," (5) *replied / was replying* one of the men. "We (6) *only make / are only making* a practice jump (*Übungssprung*)."

Station 4

Past: simple or progressive?

Name: _____

Das *Simple past* wird für Handlungen verwendet, die **abgeschlossen** sind: *She **watched** TV last night.*
Das *Past progressive* wird für Handlungen verwendet, die zu einem bestimmten Zeitpunkt noch **nicht abgeschlossen** waren: *I **was reading** a book when he came in.*

Task 1 "Track 7"

Listen to Mia's story. Write down four phrases (2x simple past and 2x past progressive).

SIMPLE PAST   PAST PROGRESSIVE

_____   _____

_____   _____

Task 2 "Track 7"

Listen to Mia's story again. Then complete the answers.

1. Was it raining that day?   No, the sun _____.
2. What did Mia do after school?   She _____ into the park.
3. Why did she go into the park?   She _____ to wait there for the bus.
4. Was she alone in the park?   No, some boys _____ football.
5. Why didn't she do homework?   She _____ tired and
                                      _____ asleep.
6. What was the man doing?   He _____ a newspaper.
7. Why did she leave the park?   The man _____ her.
8. Did the man catch up with her?   He _____ up with her at the bus stop.

Task 3

Complete the ending of Mia's story. Use the words from the box and put them into the correct past tense form.

> breathe (atmen)   say   leave (liegen lassen)   turn around (sich umdrehen)
> feel   stop

"I _____¹ a heavy hand on my shoulder. I _____² and _____³. The man _____⁴ heavily. After a moment he _____⁵, "Don't be afraid, Miss. Here are your keys. You _____⁶ them on the park bench."

Station 5

Present perfect

Name: _____

> Das *Present perfect* bildet man mit *have/has* und dem **Partizip Perfekt**:
> *I have packed* my rucksack. / *Has* Ben *arrived* yet? – No, he hasn't.
> Das *Present perfect* wird verwendet, wenn etwas irgendwann geschah und für die Gegenwart von Bedeutung ist. Der Zeitpunkt ist unbekannt oder wird nicht erwähnt.

Task 1

You want to go on a camping holiday with your friends. This is your to-do-list of jobs. Write down the jobs that your friends have done. The list of irregular verbs will help you.

1. John _____ breakfast.

2. Jim _____ a campsite.

3. Ron and Lisa _____ Rex for a walk.

4. Jim _____ the food and the drinks.

5. Lisa _____ the rucksacks.

6. Tom _____ the van.

7. Ben _____ the tent into the van.

make breakfast
choose a campsite
take Rex for a walk
buy food and drinks
pack the rucksacks
hire (*mieten*) the van
put the tent into the van

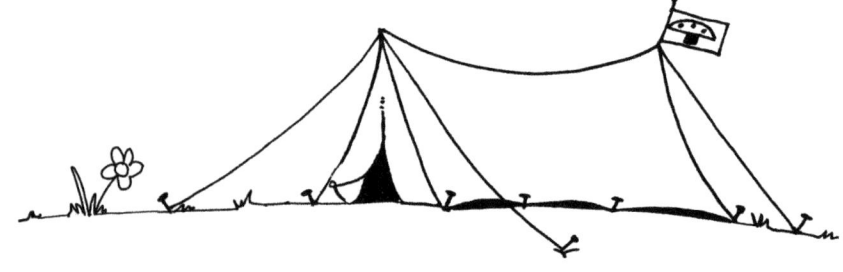

Task 2

You're a bit nervous. So you ask your friends if everything has been done.

1. John, _____ breakfast?

2. Jim, _____ a campsite?

3. Ron and Lisa, _____ Rex for a walk?

4. Jim, _____ food and drinks?

5. Lisa, _____ the rucksacks?

6. Tom, _____ the van?

7. Ben, _____ the tent into the van?

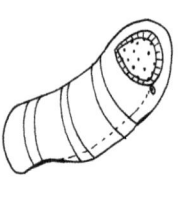

Station 6

Present perfect with *for* and *since*

Name: _____

Das deutsche **seit** wird im Englischen mit **for** oder **since** übersetzt:

I haven't seen Tina
- **for** two weeks. innerhalb eines **Zeitraums** bis jetzt
- **since** yesterday. von einem **Zeitpunkt** bis jetzt

Task 1

Put the time phrases from the box into the correct column (*Spalte*).

> two o'clock   three days   2012   two weeks   two months   Christmas
> a long time   my birthday   hours   last Tuesday

since (*seit + Zeitpunkt*)	**for** (*seit + Zeitraum*)

Task 2

At the campsite Ben meets Lin, a nice girl from the USA. Complete the dialogue. Use the verbs in brackets and the present perfect with *since* or *for*.

1. (be)   *Ben:*   _____ you _____ here _____ long?

2. (be)   *Lin:*   Yes, we' _____ here _____ Saturday.

3. (see)   *Ben:*   _____ you already _____ a lot of sights _____ you arrived?

4. (not have)   *Lin:*   No, we _____ enough time _____ last weekend.

5. (visit)   *Ben:*   _____ you ever _____ this place before?

6. (know)   *Lin:*   Yes, we' _____ this place _____ 2005.

Station 7

Past and perfect

Name:

Task 1

Highlight the correct forms.

One day Carlos and Maria (1) *were jogging / jogged* on a beach near Santa Sangria. Suddenly Carlos (2) *stepped / has stepped* on something hard in the sand. He (3) *has stopped / stopped* and (4) *was picking up / picked up* a bottle. He (5) *opened / was opening* it and (6) *has found / found* a letter inside. Carlos (7) *was showing / showed* it to Maria and they (8) *tried to / have tried to* read it. "What a pity," (9) *was saying / said* Maria. "There's sea water inside and it (10) *has made / made* some words unreadable (*unleserlich*)."

Task 2

Simple past or present perfect? Complete the letter with the correct forms of the verbs in brackets.

S.O.S – Help! Help!

We (be) _____¹ on a trip from San Domingo back to Spain. On the seventh day our ship, the Santa Maria, (sink) _____² in a terrible storm. The waves (throw) _____³ me onto the beach of a small island. I don't know what (happen) _____⁴ to my shipmates. I (be) _____⁵ on this island for three years now. I (live) _____⁶ on wild potatoes, fruit and birds' eggs. I (not see) _____⁷ any ships so far. When you find this bottle, please send help. Here's a map of the island.

Carlos and Maria (take) _____⁸ the bottle to the next police station. The officer (look) _____⁹ at the bottle and (smile) _____¹⁰. "So you (find) _____¹¹ a bottle post. Well, this is the third bottle that kids (bring) _____¹² to us today."

Station 8

Mixed tenses

Task 1

Problems at the campsite. Complete the sentences with the correct form of the verb.

1. Simple present: Lin _____ (have) a problem.
2. Present progressive: She _____ (look) for her parents.
3. Simple past: She _____ (go) to the camp restaurant.
4. Past progressive: Ben _____ (have) his breakfast there.
5. Present perfect: "_____ you _____ (see) my parents?" Lin asked him.

Task 2

Where are Lin's parents? Put the verbs in brackets into the correct form.

When Ben saw Lin five hours later, she (cry) _____ ¹.

Ben: Why (you/cry) _____ ²?

Lin: I (not/can/find) _____ ³ my parents.

Ben: (you/ask) _____ ⁴ at the reception yet?

Lin: Yes, I have. They (not/see) _____ ⁵ them at all today.

Ben: And when (you/last/see) _____ ⁶ them?

Lin: Last night, when we (go) _____ ⁷ to bed.

Ben: So they (not be) _____ ⁸ in the tent when you got up?

Lin: No, but they (talk) _____ ⁹ outside.

Ben: I think they just (drive) _____ ¹⁰ to the market to buy things.

Task 3

The father's story. Highlight the correct verb forms.

We woke up very early. Lin (1) *has still been sleeping/was still sleeping,* so we (2) *went/were going* to town by car to buy food and drinks. We (3) *left/were leaving* the supermarket when a man on a bike (4) *overtook/has overtaken* (überholen) us and (5) *was snatching/snatched* (schnappen) my wife's handbag with our passports and the car keys in it. We (6) *reported/were reporting* the theft (Diebstahl) to the police and (7) *have had to/had to* come back by taxi.

Station 9

Past participles

Name:

Das Partizip Perfekt (*past participle*) ist die dritte Form des Verbs: *take – took – **taken***.

Task 1

Write the perfect participle forms of the verbs into the crossword puzzle. Look up any verbs that you don't know in an English-German dictionary.

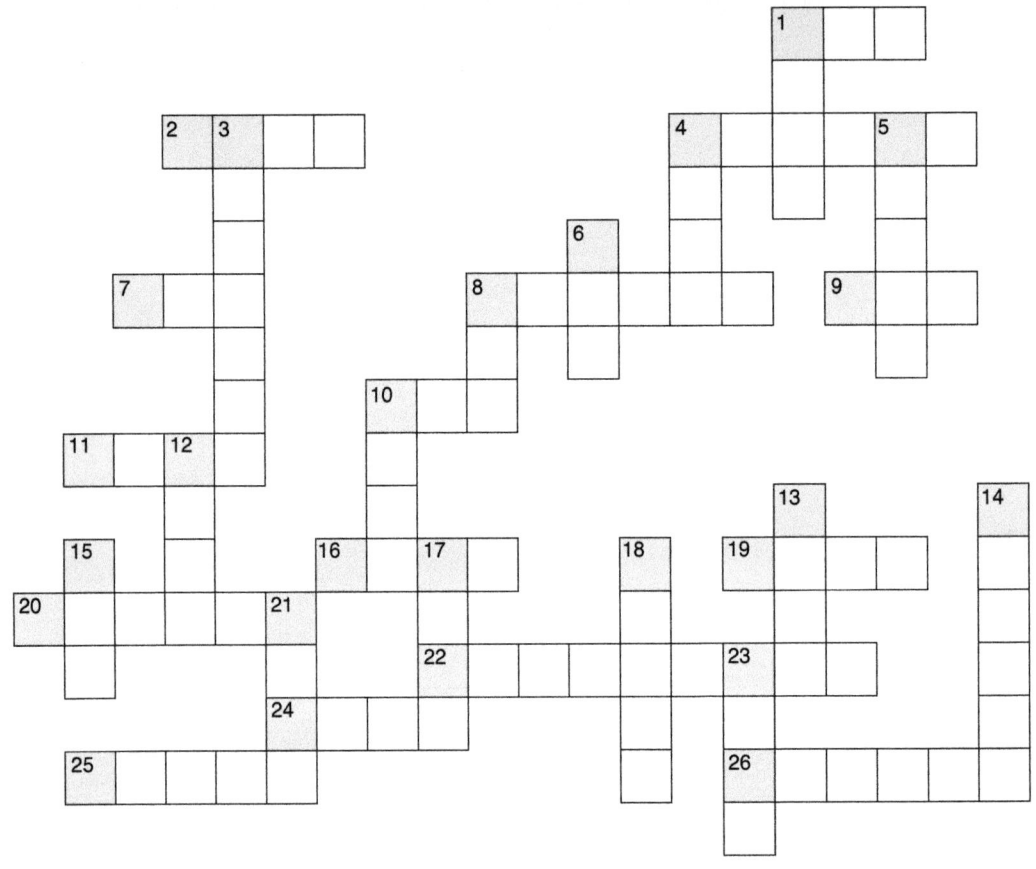

Across
1. put, 2. swim, 4. drive, 7. sit, 8. choose, 9. feed, 10. get, 11. wear, 16. hold, 19. say, 20. catch, 22. forget, 24. lend, 25. find, 26. ride

Down
1. pay, 3. write, 4. do, 5. eat, 6. win, 8. cut, 10. go, 12. ring, 13. make, 14. speak, 15. have, 17. leave, 18. know, 21. tell, 23. tear

Task 2

Look at the example. Then find the other rhyming pairs.

> run had flown read got
> come met caught done felt

> gun pad own belt ton rum
> bed hot wet sort

run – gun

Station 1

Comparison of adjectives

Name:

Task "Track 8"

Listen and fill in the adjectives used to describe the animals. Then listen again and complete the table with the comparative forms of the adjectives, for example *small – smaller – (the) smallest; intelligent – more intelligent – most intelligent*.
(poisonous = *giftig*)

1. Willy the whale

   big

   slow

2. Olga the orca

3. Dolly the dolphin

4. Leo the lion

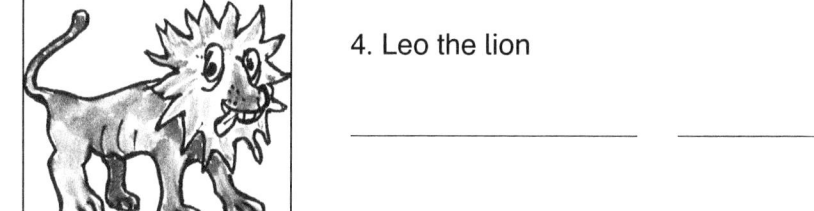

5. Gary the gorilla

6. Vera the viper

Station 2

Comparison of adverbs

Name:

> **Adverbien der Art und Weise** (*Adverbs of manner*)
> Adverbien, die auf **-ly** enden, bilden die Steigerungsformen mit **more** und **most**.
> Haben Adjektiv und Adverb die gleiche Form, steigert man das Adverb wie das Adjektiv mit **-er** und **-est**: *fast, faster, fastest.*

Task

Read the explanation above and then complete the following list. Look up any adjectives you don't know in an English-German dictionary.

ADJECTIVE	ADVERB	COMPARISONS
1. slow	slowly	more slowly, most slowly
2. fast		
3. dangerous		
4. playful		
5. clever		
6. strong		
7. hungry		
8. nasty		
9. good		
10. angry		
11. poisonous		
12. hard		
13. soft		
14. expensive		
15. quiet		
16. loud		
17. careful		
18. careless		
19. rude		
20. bad		

Mixed bag

Station 3

Present and future

Name:

Zusammen mit einer Zeitangabe können *Simple present* und *Present progressive* für Pläne (z. B. Fahrpläne und Programme) verwendet werden: *The tour **starts** tomorrow. At around 12:30 we're stopping for lunch at the Red Fox Inn.*

Task 1 "Track 9"

Look at the questions below. What information do you need for the answers? Listen to Part 1 of the class trip and make notes. Then answer the questions.

1. What's happening tomorrow? – The pupils _____ on a class trip.

2. Where are they going? – They _____.

3. Where do the pupils meet? – They _____.

4. When does the class meet? – The class _____.

5. What do they have to wear? – They _____
   _____.

6. What do they have to bring? – They _____.

Task 2 "Track 10"

Now listen to Part 2 of the class trip and fill in all the times in the schedule below. Then listen to Part 2 again and complete the list of activities.

	TIMES	ACTIVITIES
1.	8:15 a.m.	_____ in front of school. Don't be late!
2.		Coach _____. Find a seat quickly.
3.		Coach _____. We won't wait for late pupils!
4.		_____. We have 20 minutes.
5.		We _____ at the cathedral in York.
6.		The guided tour _____. It takes one hour.
7.		We _____ up outside the cathedral.
8.	11:35 a.m. – 2 p.m.	FREE ACTIVITIES + LUNCH
9.		Jorvik Viking Centre tour _____.
10.		_____ outside the centre and walk back to the coach.
11.		_____ the journey back. We want to arrive at 6 p.m.

Station 4

The *will*-future

Name: _____

Mit dem *Will-future* kann man über die Zukunft berichten, z. B. über eine Vereinbarung: *Don't worry. I won't tell your mum.*
Merke: Meist wird die Kurzform **'ll/won't** benutzt. Mit der Langform **will/will not** wird die Aussage betont.

Task 1

Look at the list of jobs. What do they say?

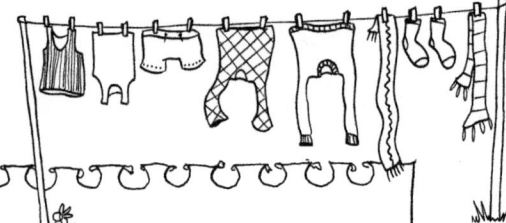

```
WEEKLY JOBS
Mum + Dad    do the shopping, do the driving
Mum          do the cooking, do the washing (Wäsche waschen)
Dad          wash the car, do the gardening
Sue          make the beds, vacuum (staubsaugen) the rooms
Ben          feed the dog, take it for a walk
```

1. *Mum and Dad:* <u>We'll do the shopping and the driving.</u>

2. *Mum:* _____

3. *Dad:* _____

4. *Sue:* _____

5. *Ben:* _____

Verwende **will** und **won't** für spontane Reaktionen und Entschlüsse: *Oh no, it's raining. I will stay at home.*
Merke: Die Langformen **will** und **will not** betonen die Aussage.

Task 2

Match the sentences (1–6) with the responses (*Reaktionen*) (A–F).

1. You're talking absolute nonsense.
2. I think Fluffy is hungry.
3. This is a boring programme.
4. These biscuits are very tasty.
5. Can you give me some money?
6. I want you to tidy up your room.

A) Good. I'll bake (*backen*) some more.
B) No, I will not give you more money!
C) OK, I won't say another word.
D) Yes, I'll tidy it up after school.
E) I'll give her some cat food.
F) I'll find something better.

1 [ ] 2 [ ] 3 [ ] 4 [ ] 5 [ ] 6 [ ]

Station 5

The *going to*-future

Name:

> Verwende das *Going to-future* für Ereignisse, die bald oder wahrscheinlich (nicht) geschehen werden: *The train isn't slowing down. It **isn't going to stop** at this station.*

Task 1

Match the pictures (1–6) to the sentences (A–F).

1. Ann: _____
2. Mabel and Fred: _____
3. Roy: _____
4. Harriet: _____
5. Mike and Diana: _____
6. Tom: _____

A) We're going to eat lots of popcorn and enjoy a horror film.

B) I'm going to take out the rubbish (*Müll*) and then sit in the garden and read a book.

C) I'm going to catch a really big fish and give it to my Mum.

D) I'm going to miss this ball, but I'm not going to miss the next one!

E) I'm going to take Rex for a long walk and then we're going to have a picnic.

F) We're going to clean the wall and then we're going to paint it blue.

Task 2

Complete the questions with two of these words: *who, what, is, are*.

1. _____ going to miss the ball?   – Our goalkeeper!
2. _____ the dog going to catch?   – The frisbee.
3. _____ Mabel and Fred going to visit?   – Their grandma.
4. _____ Fred and Mabel going to eat?   – Banana sandwiches.
5. _____ going to go shopping with you?   – Fred and Mabel.

Station 6

Future with *going to* or *will*

Name:

Verwende *going to*, wenn etwas **geplant** ist oder **wahrscheinlich bald** geschehen wird:
We're going to play football on Saturday. / Look at the sky. It's going to snow soon.
Ansonsten benutze das *will*-future.

Task 1

Complete the sentences with the *will*-future.

1. _____ (you/go shopping) with me tomorrow morning?

2. Yes, and _____ (I/call) Susan and ask her to come, too.

3. Susan _____ (not/be) in. She's on holiday in Turkey.

Task 2

Complete the sentences with the correct future forms.

Andy: I think (I/go) _____ [1] for a short walk.

Dora: Look at those dark clouds. (it/rain) _____ [2] in the next few minutes. If you go out now, (you/get) _____ [3] wet.

Andy: OK. (I/put on) _____ [4] my raincoat and (I/take) _____ [5] an umbrella with me, too.

Dora: When (you/be) _____ [6] back?

Andy: I'm not sure. Why?

Dora: (I/cook) _____ [7] a meal in half an hour.

Andy: Oh! What (you/make) _____ [8]?

Dora: Your favourite meal – fish and chips.

Andy: Oh great. (I/be) _____ [9] back home in twenty minutes or so.

Dora: OK, but (you/not be) _____ [10] late, will you?

Andy: Don't worry. (I/not miss) _____ [11] my favourite meal!

Dora: Good, then (I/see) _____ [12] you soon, won't I?

Station 7

Conditional sentences, type 1

Name:

> Die Verben im **Nebensatz** mit *if* stehen im *Simple present*.
> Die Verben im **Hauptsatz** stehen entweder im *Simple present* oder im *Will-future*:
> *If you **need** help, you **should ask** your teacher.*
> *If it **rains** tomorrow, I **will go** to the cinema.*

Task 1

Join the two halves of these conditional sentences.

1. If you take a number 8 bus,
2. If you leave now,
3. If you want to play well,
4. If you go shopping,
5. If you see the lion first,
6. If you're hungry,
7. If you hear strange noises (*Geräusche*),
8. If the telephone rings,
9. If the lion sees you first,

A) can you buy some eggs?
B) please don't go down into the cellar (*Keller*).
C) it will take you to the station.
D) there's a meat pie (*Fleischpastete*) in the fridge.
E) you must train regularly.
F) please don't pick up.
G) you won't miss the bus.
H) run as fast as you can.
I) stand very still and be very quiet.

1 ☐ 2 ☐ 3 ☐ 4 ☐ 5 ☐ 6 ☐ 7 ☐ 8 ☐ 9 ☐

Task 2

The following conditional sentences are type 1. Fill in the correct form of the verbs.

1. If anybody _____ (call), tell them I'll be back in an hour.

2. She must train more often if she _____ (want) to play well.

3. Yes, I _____ (join) the team if the trainer invites me.

4. If he _____ (not want to) listen, nobody can help him.

5. What do we do if the crocodile _____ (get) hungry?

6. If it _____ (snow) again, can we go skiing?

7. If Ted doesn't train more often, he _____ (never get) better.

8. If Rex is hungry, he _____ (eat) anything!

9. Sue will be angry if Mark _____ (not call) her soon.

10. If the sentence _____ (start) with *if*, you must use a comma.

Station 8

Present perfect – word order

Name: _____

Task 1

Fill the gaps with the missing words below, but in the correct word order.

Mrs Bradford's washing machine _____¹ again.

She _____² the repair service and they _____

_____³. They _____

_____⁴ a repairman, probably sometime around two o'clock that afternoon. After the call,

Mrs Bradford remembers that _____⁵ an appointment

(*Termin*) with her dentist for one o'clock that afternoon. If it takes longer than an hour, she might

miss the repairman. And if she's at the dentist's, how will she know if the repairman _____

_____⁶ at her home? But Mrs Bradford _____

_____⁷ before and she knows what she has to do.

She writes this message (*Nachricht*) and tapes (*festkleben*) it to her front door:

1. broken / down / has
2. already / has / phoned
3. back / called / have / her / just
4. have / promised / send / to
5. already / has / made / she
6. already / called (*vorbeischauen*) / hasn't
7. had / has / problem / this

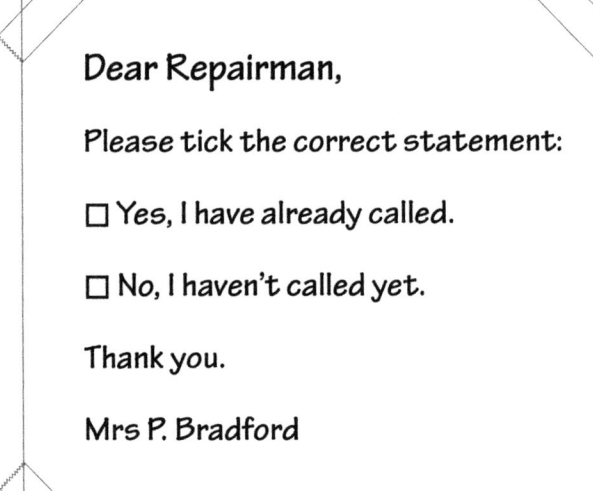

Dear Repairman,

Please tick the correct statement:

☐ Yes, I have already called.

☐ No, I haven't called yet.

Thank you.

Mrs P. Bradford

Task 2 "Track 11"

Now listen to the story on the CD and check your answers.

Station 9

A taste of phrasal verbs

Name:

Task 1

Match the English phrases (1–4) with the German translations (A–D).

1. to ask after sb
2. to ask for sth
3. to ask for sb
4. to ask about sth

A) *jdn sprechen wollen/jdn verlangen*
B) *etw wissen wollen über …*
C) *sich nach jdm erkundigen*
D) *um etw bitten; etw verlangen*

1 ☐   2 ☐   3 ☐   4 ☐

Task 2

Use the following switchboard to translate the German sentences below into English.

| A neighbour
A hotel guest
A police officer
My mother
My parents
My doctor
The train conductor
I | asked | about
after
for | me.
my ticket.
my parents.
a telephone book for London.
the manager.
the price of a daily return ticket.
my hobbies.
the class trip. |

1. Ein Nachbar erkundigte sich nach meinen Eltern.
   _____

2. Ein Hotelgast verlangte ein Telefonbuch von London.
   _____

3. Eine Polizistin wollte mich sprechen.
   _____

4. Meine Mutter verlangte, die Chefin zu sprechen.
   _____

5. Meine Eltern erkundigten sich über die Klassenfahrt.
   _____

6. Die Ärztin wollte etwas über meine Hobbys wissen.
   _____

7. Die Zugbegleiterin verlangte meine Fahrkarte.
   _____

8. Ich fragte nach dem Preis einer Tagesrückfahrkarte.
   _____

Station 10

A mixed bag of tenses

Name: _____

Task 1

Complete the interview with the correct tenses: simple present, present progressive, simple past, past progressive, present perfect and *going to*-future.

Anne: Excuse me, I (interview) _____¹ tourists for our local newspaper. May I ask you a few questions?

Chris: With pleasure. I (never / be) _____² interviewed before by such a pretty reporter.

Anne: How (you / like) _____³ our town?

Chris: I think it's fantastic. I (have) _____⁴ great fun.

Anne: And how long (you / stay) _____⁵?

Chris: I (stay) _____⁶ for another day.

Anne: What (you / see) _____⁷ in Heidelberg so far?

Chris: Well, first I (go) _____⁸ to see an old friend who (live) _____⁹ here.

I (just / do) _____¹⁰ some shopping when you stopped me.

Anne: I see. You (carry) _____¹¹ a heavy shopping bag. May I ask what you (buy) _____¹²?

Chris: I (find) _____¹³ an antique statue of the god Neptune.

Anne: How interesting! And where (you / find) _____¹⁴ it?

Chris: I don't remember exactly. That must (be) _____¹⁵ in one of these souvenir shops. A surprise for my girlfriend, you know.

Anne: I have a surprise for you, too. I'm a police officer. Please, follow me to the police station. You (steal) _____¹⁶ this statue from the museum.

Task 2

First check your answers. Then practise the interview with a partner.

Station 1: Basic grammatical terms — page 7

Task 1

1. hungry
2. badly
3. the
4. a/an
5. and
6. he
7. his
8. dance
9. must
10. cup
11. with

Task 2

1. D
2. F
3. B
4. H
5. G
6. E
7. A
8. C

Station 2: Pronouns (1) — page 8

Task 1

you – you – your
she – her – her
we – us – our
he – him – his
it – it – its
they – them – their

Task 2

3. they
4. me
5. He
6. she
7. him
8. her
9. them
10. My
11. they
12. us
13. We
14. she
15. them

Station 3: Adjectives — page 9

Task 1

2. fresh orange juice
3. crispy croissants
4. interesting video film
5. white hat and coat
6. yellow boots
7. giant mixer
8. useful brochures

Task 2

Individual solutions

Station 4: Adverbs (1) — page 10

Task 1

adjectives: young, same (2x), loud, poor, bad, long, small, ruined, new
adverbs: easily, loudly, quickly, roughly, slowly, angrily, carefully

Task 2

1. Onkel Harry riecht schlecht.
2. Onkel Harry kann schlecht riechen.

Task 3

1. Dad <u>often</u> reads the morning newspaper at breakfast.
2. Mum <u>sometimes</u> asks him for the page with the crossword puzzle.
3. I don't <u>usually</u> eat more than a slice of toast for breakfast.

Station 5: Modal auxiliaries — page 11/12

Task 1

1. Kann/Darf
2. kann
3. kannst/darfst
4. wird
5. Darf
6. müssen
7. brauchen nicht

Task 2

1. Can he dance the tango? – Yes, he can.
2. Can he cook meals? – No, he can't.
3. Can he paint pictures? – Yes, he can.
4. Can he catch cats? – No, he can't.
5. Can he eat anything? – Yes, he can.
6. Can he do Maths homework? – No, he can't.

Task 3

1. C
2. B
3. A
4. B
5. A
6. C

Task 4

1. E
2. G
3. F
4. A
5. D
6. C
7. H
8. B

Task 5

1. Can, can't
2. Will, won't
3. Must, must

Task 6

1. You have to sit here.
2. Why do we have to sit here?
3. Simon has to try harder.
4. Simon has to do his homework.
5. Does his Mum have to help him?

Station 6: Prepositions — page 13

Task 1

1. in
2. on
3. at
4. in
5. in
6. in
7. at
8. in
9. on

Task 2

1. under
2. between
3. behind
4. in
5. on
6. in front of

Station 7: Irregular plurals — page 14

Task 1

Across
2. wife
4. knife
5. person
8. sheep
9. tooth

Down
1. man
2. woman
3. child
6. pony
7. fish

Station 7: Irregular plurals — page 14

In the crossword puzzle:

Across
2. wives   4. knives   5. people   8. sheep
9. teeth

Down
1. men   2. women   3. children   6. ponies
7. fish

Task 2
1. wolf, wolves   2. mouse, mice   3. scarf, scarves

Station 8: Simple present — page 15

Task 1
2. get   3. call   4. jumps   5. says
6. don't … speak   7. go   8. follows   9. have
10. brush   11. put   12. jumps   13. sits
14. barks   15. tries   16. don't … wear   17. walks
18. have   19. locks

Task 2

Individual solutions

Task 3

usually   always   usually   often
never

Station 9: Questions and short answers — page 16

Task 1
1. it isn't   2. it doesn't   3. it doesn't   4. it doesn't
5. it hasn't   6. I do   7. goldfish, it is

Task 2

Individual solutions

Task 3
1. Is, he is
2. Do you, I don't
3. Are his, they aren't
4. Are, they are
5. Has he, he has
6. Do you, I do
7. Are you, I'm not / Do you know, I don't

Station 10: Present progressive — page 17

Task
1. I'm holding a kitten.
2. I'm feeding the kitten from a bottle.
3. She's driving a tractor.
4. They're looking for eggs.
5. He's milking a cow.
6. They're riding ponies.
7. He's chasing birds.

Station 11: Questions and question words — page 18

Task 1

1. How
2. Whose
3. What
4. Where
5. Why
6. When
7. Who

Task 2

A 2, B 7, C 6   D 9, E 5, F 1   G 4, H 3, I 8

Task 3

1. Who helps Hagrid?
2. Who does Hagrid help?
3. Who do all pupils like?

Station 1: Grammatical terms — page 19

Task 1

1. E
2. J
3. I
4. F
5. A
6. D
7. B
8. G
9. C
10. H

Task 2

1. D
2. G
3. A
4. F
5. H
6. C
7. E
8. B

Station 2: The present tense of *be* — page 20

Task 1

1. I'm
2. she isn't
3. we aren't
4. we are
5. we aren't
6. I'm not

Task 2

1. Am, are, aren't
2. Is, he is, he isn't
3. Are, we are, we aren't
4. Are, they are, they aren't
5. Is, it is, it isn't
6. Are, I am, I'm not

Task 3

Musterdialog:

1. Are you new in our class? – Yes, I am. / No, I'm not.
2. Are you Greek? – Yes, I am. / No, I'm not.
3. Are your parents from Greece? – Yes, they are. / No, they aren't.
4. Is your sister at our school, too? – Yes, she is. / No, she isn't.
5. Is she older than you? – Yes, she is. / No, she isn't.
6. Are you good at English? – Yes, I am. / No, I'm not.

Station 3: The simple past forms of *be* — page 21

Task 1

1. Were, was, weren't
2. Were, were, weren't
3. Was, was, wasn't
4. Were, were, weren't
5. Was, were, weren't
6. Were, were, weren't

Task 2

1. Were, were, weren't
2. Were, weren't, were
3. Was, was, wasn't
4. Was, wasn't, was
5. Are, are, 'm not, is

Station 4: Present: simple or progressive? (1) — page 22

Task 1

1. is going, walks
2. runs, buys, carries
3. is practising, goes, buys
4. is still sleeping, is reading, doesn't do, reads

Task 2

1. is staying
2. comes
3. are visiting
4. walk
5. have
6. stop
7. says

Station 5: Imperatives — page 23

Task

1. Turn
2. Don't turn
3. Don't smoke
4. leave
5. Don't picnic
6. Put
7. Take
8. Let's
9. keep
10. Don't wear
11. let's
12. turn, Think
13. Show

Station 6: Simple past (1) — page 24

Task 1

1. right
2. wrong
3. right
4. wrong

Task 2

Group 1: happened, jumped, opened, played
Group 2: planned, spotted, swapped, tripped
Group 3: copied, hurried, tidied, worried

Task 3

1. went
2. bought
3. came
4. saw
5. thought
6. had
7. drew

Station 7: Simple past – irregular verbs — page 25

Task 1

1. go, went
2. does, did
3. rides, rode
4. find, found
5. throw, threw
6. teaches, taught
7. steal, stole
8. speaks, spoke
9. says, said
10. leave, left
11. sees, saw

Task 2

1. rode
2. went
3. left
4. stole
5. wasn't
6. went
7. threw
8. caught
9. found
10. had

Station 8: Pronouns (2) — page 26

Task 1

1. C 2. D 3. A 4. B

Task 2

1. me, mine
2. you, their
3. them, we
4. our, theirs
5. him
6. It, it, hers
7. I, my, you, it

Station 9: Adverbs (2) — page 27

Task 1

adverbs of time: 3 *adverbs of frequency:* 2 *adverbs of manner:* 1 *adverbs of place:* 4

Task 2

Individual solutions

Task 3

1. softly, hard
2. Yesterday
3. here
4. in front of
5. never
6. badly
7. well, soon
8. now, later

Station 10: Adjectives and adverbs — page 28

Task 1

1. in front of
2. out
3. quickly
4. straight
5. carefully
6. anywhere
7. angry
8. angrily
9. quietly
10. clever

Task 2

adjectives: 7. angry, 10. clever
adverbs: 1. in front of, 2. out, 3. quickly, 4. straight, 5. carefully, 6. anywhere, 8. angrily, 9. quietly

Task 3

1. You must carry a bottle of TNT <u>carefully</u>.
2. I went to a rock concert in the park <u>yesterday</u>. / <u>Yesterday</u> I went to a rock concert in the park.
3. I don't <u>usually</u> wear green socks with blue shoes.
4. The ball rolled <u>straight</u> across the road.

Station 11: *Some/any* — page 29

Task 1

1. any 2. any 3. some 4. any
5. any 6. some 7. some 8. Some

Task 2

1. somewhere
2. anywhere
3. anyone/anybody
4. anything
5. anything
6. someone/somebody
7. something

Station 12: Simple past (2) — page 30/31

Task 1

1. fest, Firma
2. (Zeit) verbringen, (Geld) ausgeben
3. spionieren, ausspähen
4. wispern, flüstern
5. Erstaunen, Überraschung
6. Türstufe, Türschwelle
7. berühmt, weltbekannt

Task 2

1. drive, drove
2. finds, found
3. hears, heard
4. hold, held
5. keep, kept
6. knows, knew
7. make, made
8. says, said
9. sees, saw
10. spends, spent
11. spies, spied
12. think, thought
13. wakes, woke up

Task 3

1. were
2. was
3. made
4. had
5. told
6. didn't work
7. spent
8. spied
9. knew
10. had
11. kept
12. woke
13. saw
14. heard
15. drove
16. thought
17. found
18. didn't wake up
19. slept
20. held
21. didn't know
22. was
23. was

Station 1: Past, present and future — page 32

Task 1

PAST: 2, 7, 13, 16, 18
PRESENT (+ PERFECT): 4, 5, 6, 8, 12, 15
FUTURE: 3, 9, 10, 11, 14, 17

Task 2

1. G
2. F
3. E
4. B
5. A
6. C
7. H
8. D

Station 2: Present: simple or progressive? (2) — page 33

Task

2. He usually makes breakfast at 10 a.m., but today he's having breakfast at the pub.
3. He usually flies around on his broom at 11 a.m., but today he's writing a letter to Harry Potter.
4. He usually cooks lunch at 1 p.m., but today he's eating at the Witches Club.
5. He usually reads magic books at 2 p.m., but today he's creating magic flowers.
6. He usually does magic at 3 p.m., but today he's taking dragon Bert for a walk.
7. He usually teaches magic at school at 4 p.m., but today Bert and Merlin are playing tennis.
8. He usually dances with witches at 5 p.m., but today he's preparing a party.
9. He usually reads a horror story at 6 p.m., but today he's creating flying bikes.
10. He usually cleans his broom at 7 p.m., but today Bert and Merlin are riding their bikes.

Station 3: Past progressive — page 34

Task 1

1. John and Jim were playing poker.
2. Frank was polishing his saddle.
3. Mac says he was cleaning his revolvers.
4. Ron and Harry say, "We were drinking beer."
5. The cowboy was playing the piano.
6. The horse says, "I was waiting outside."

Task 2

1. was circling
2. were getting ready
3. shouted
4. aren't wearing
5. replied
6. are only making

Station 4: Past: simple or progressive? — page 35

Task 1

Individual solutions

Task 2

1. was shining
2. went
3. wanted
4. were playing
5. was, fell
6. was reading
7. was watching
8. caught

Task 3

1. felt
2. stopped
3. turned around
4. was breathing
5. said
6. left

Station 5: Present perfect — page 36

Task 1

1. has made
2. has chosen
3. have taken
4. has bought
5. has packed
6. has hired
7. has put

Task 2

1. have you made
2. have you chosen
3. have you taken
4. have you bought
5. have you packed
6. have you hired
7. have you put

Station 6: Present perfect with *for* and *since* — page 37

Task 1

since	*for*
two o'clock	three days
last Tuesday	two weeks
Christmas	a long time
my birthday	two months
2012	hours

Task 2

1. <u>Have</u> you <u>been</u> here <u>for</u> long?
2. Yes, we<u>'ve been</u> here <u>since</u>Saturday.
3. <u>Have</u> you already <u>seen</u> a lot of sights <u>since</u> you arrived?
4. No, we <u>haven't had</u> enough time <u>since</u> last weekend.
5. <u>Have</u> you ever <u>visited</u> this place before?
6. Yes, we<u>'ve known</u> this place <u>since</u> 2005.

Station 7: Past and perfect — page 38

Task 1

1. were jogging
2. stepped
3. stopped
4. picked up
5. opened
6. found
7. showed
8. tried to
9. said
10. has made

Task 2

1. were
2. sank
3. threw
4. happened / has happened
5. have been
6. have lived
7. haven't seen
8. took
9. looked
10. smiled
11. have found
12. have brought

Station 8: Mixed tenses — page 39

Task 1

1. has
2. 's looking
3. went
4. was having
5. Have … seen

Task 2

1. was crying
2. are you crying
3. can't find
4. Have you asked
5. haven't seen
6. did you last see
7. went / were going
8. weren't
9. were talking
10. drove

Task 3

1. was still sleeping
2. went
3. were leaving
4. overtook
5. snatched
6. reported
7. had to

Station 9: Past participles — page 40

Task 1

Across

1. put
2. swum
4. driven
7. sat
8. chosen
9. fed
10. got
11. worn
16. held
19. said
20. caught
22. forgotten
24. lent
25. found
26. ridden

Down

1. paid
3. written
4. done
5. eaten
6. won
8. cut
10. gone
12. rung
13. made
14. spoken
15. had
17. left
18. known
21. told
23. torn

Task 2

come – rum
had – pad
met – wet
flown – own
caught – sort
read – bed
done – ton
got – hot
felt – belt

Station 1: Comparison of adjectives — page 41

Task

1. big, bigger, (the) biggest
   slow, slower, (the) slowest
2. fast, faster, (the) fastest
   dangerous, more dangerous, (the) most dangerous
3. playful, more playful, (the) most playful
   clever, cleverer, (the) cleverest
4. strong, stronger, (the) strongest
   hungry, hungrier, (the) hungriest
5. hairy, hairier, (the) hairiest
   good, better, (the) best
6. angry, angrier, (the) angriest
   poisonous, more poisonous, (the) most poisonous

Station 2: Comparison of adverbs — page 42

Task

2. fast – faster, fastest
3. dangerously – more dangerously, most dangerously
4. playfully – more playfully, most playfully
5. cleverly – more cleverly, most cleverly
6. strongly – more strongly, most strongly
7. hungrily – more hungrily, most hungrily
8. nastily – more nastily, most nastily
9. well – better, best
10. angrily – more angrily, most angrily
11. poisonously – more poisonously, most poisonously
12. hard – harder, hardest (Be careful: hardly = *kaum*)
13. softly – more softly, most softly
14. expensively – more expensively, most expensively
15. quietly – more quietly, most quietly
16. loudly – more loudly, most loudly
17. carefully – more carefully, most carefully
18. carelessly – more carelessly, most carelessly
19. rudely – more rudely, most rudely
20. badly – worse, worst

Station 3: Present and future — page 43

Task 1

1. The pupils are going on a class trip.
2. They're going to York.
3. They meet in front of the school.
4. The class meets at 8:15 (a.m./the next morning).
5. They have to wear a raincoat or an umbrella and sensible shoes.
6. They have to bring something to eat and drink.

Task 2

1. Meet
2. 8:20 a.m., arrives
3. 8:30 a.m., leaves
4. 9:00 a.m., Picnic breakfast
5. 10:15 a.m., arrive
6. 10:30 a.m., starts
7. 11:30 a.m., meet
9. 2:00 p.m., starts
10. 4:00 p.m., Meet
11. 4:15 p.m., Start

Station 4: The *will*-future — page 44

Task 1

2. I'll do the cooking and the washing.
3. I'll wash the car and do the gardening.
4. I'll make the beds and vacuum the rooms.
5. I'll feed the dog and take it for a walk.

Task 2

1. C
2. E
3. F
4. A
5. B
6. D

Station 5: The *going to*-future — page 45

Task 1

1. D
2. A
3. C
4. E
5. F
6. B

Task 2

1. Who is
2. What is
3. Who are
4. What are
5. Who is

Station 6: Future with *going to* or *will* — page 46

Task 1

1. Will you go shopping
2. I'll call
3. won't be

Task 2

1. I'll go
2. It's going to rain
3. you'll get
4. I'll put on
5. I'll take
6. will you be
7. I'm going to cook
8. are you going to make
9. I'll be
10. you won't be
11. I won't miss
12. I'll see

Station 7: Conditional sentences, type 1 — page 47

Task 1

1. C
2. G
3. E
4. A
5. H
6. D
7. B
8. F
9. I

Task 2

1. calls
2. wants
3. 'll join
4. doesn't want to
5. gets
6. snows
7. 'll never get
8. 'll eat
9. doesn't call
10. starts

Station 8: Present perfect – word order — page 48

Task 1

1. has broken down
2. has already phoned
3. have just called her back
4. have promised to send
5. she has already made
6. hasn't already called
7. has had this problem

Station 9: A taste of phrasal verbs — page 49

Task 1

1. C   2. D   3. A   4. B

Task 2

1. A neighbour asked after my parents.
2. A hotel guest asked for a telephone book of London.
3. A police officer asked for me.
4. My mother asked for the manager.
5. My parents asked about the class trip.
6. The doctor asked about my hobbies.
7. The train conductor asked for my ticket.
8. I asked about the price of a daily return ticket.

Station 10: A mixed bag of tenses — page 50

Task 1 and 2

1. 'm interviewing
2. 've never been
3. do you like
4. 'm having
5. are you going to stay / are you staying
6. 'm going to stay / 'm staying
7. have you seen
8. went
9. lives
10. was just doing
11. 're carrying
12. 've bought
13. found
14. did you find
15. have been
16. stole

Transcripts of the listening comprehension texts

Track 1 – Station 3: Adjectives, Tasks 1 and 2 (Basics, S. 9)

Our class trip is a visit to a chocolate factory. A young woman meets us in front of the factory. Her name is Mrs Taylor and she's our guide. She talks to us and our teacher. She's very friendly. Our teacher likes her. Mrs Taylor takes us to a big room. It's the factory canteen. She says we can have a quick breakfast before we start our tour. I drink two big glasses of fresh orange juice because I'm thirsty. I eat some croissants, too. They're warm and crispy. I love crispy croissants. Then we watch a video film about the factory. It's interesting, but I miss some of it because I have to go to the toilet.
Mrs Taylor tells us that in a chocolate factory everything must be very clean. Visitors must be very clean, too. We all get a white hat and a white coat. We must take off our shoes, too. Mrs Taylor gives us special yellow boots. We go onto the factory floor. We stop in front of a big machine. Mrs Taylor tells us that it makes the chocolate. We walk up some stairs and look inside. It's a giant mixer. At the end of the tour, Mrs Taylor gives us lots of brochures. They're useful because they have all the information I need for my report. We all get a bag of chocolates, too.

Track 2 – Station 9: Simple present, Task 2 (Basics, S. 15)

The alarm clock rings. I get up and call Rex, my dog. A big, red cat jumps out of my bed and says, "Hello, Tom." Very strange! Cats don't usually speak English.
I go to the bathroom. The big cat follows me. I always have a shower and brush my teeth first thing in the morning. But the door is locked. So I put on my shirt and my socks. Very strange – they are much too big.
The big, red cat jumps onto the chair and sits down on my jeans. It barks just like Rex, "Wuff, wuff, wuff". Then it tries to get into my jeans. Very strange! Cats don't usually wear jeans.
I go downstairs to the kitchen – the cat walks in front of me. We often have breakfast in the kitchen. But the door is locked. Mum never locks the kitchen door. Very strange!
There's something wrong with the house today. I go back to my room and sit down on the bed. Suddenly there's a loud knock at the door and I hear my mother shout, "Tom, get up! You're late. Hurry, it's already seven o'clock."

Track 3 – Station 10: Present progressive, Task (Basics, S. 17)

My name is Ellen. I've got a fantastic new camera and I take photos every day. Here are some photos from our visit to the Children's farm zoo. It's really exciting.
In photo one I am holding a kitten. Isn't she sweet?
And here's photo two. Now I'm feeding the kitten from a bottle. It's special milk for baby cats. She likes it very much.
The girl in photo three is Jane Cox. She works on the farm. She's driving a tractor.
Tim and his sister Sally are here, too. In photo four they're looking for eggs.
And in photo five you can see the farmer's son Bob. Isn't he good-looking? He's milking a cow.
The two girls in picture six are from Germany – Lisa and Anna. They are riding ponies for the first time.
Lisa and Anna have got a big black dog. His name is Pinkie. In photo seven he's chasing birds in a field.

Track 4 – Station 6: Simple past (1), Task 3 (Mixed grammar, S. 24)

Mr Dobbs had mice in his kitchen. So he went to town and bought a mousetrap. When he came home, he saw that he had no cheese for the trap. "What can I do?" he thought. So he drew a nice picture of a piece of cheese and coloured it yellow. Then he put the picture in the mousetrap. The next morning when he looked at the trap, he got a great surprise. Next to his picture of the cheese was a nice picture of a mouse.

Track 5 – Station 7: Simple past – irregular verbs, Task 2 (Mixed grammar, S. 25)

One day famous Wild Bill Hickcock rode into Silvercity and went into the bar for a drink. When Wild Bill left the saloon, he found that his horse was no longer there.
He went back into the bar, threw his guns into the air, caught them above his head, fired a shot into the mirror and said, "Who stole my horse?" Nobody spoke. "Well," said Wild Bill, "I'll have another beer and if my horse isn't back by the time I finish, I'll do what I did in Texas last month. And I don't like to do what I did in Texas last month."
Everybody was frightened. Wild Bill had another beer, left the bar and saw his horse standing outside. The barman followed the cowboy and asked, "Say, Bill, before you go, what did you do in Texas last month?" And Wild Bill replied, "Nothing, I had to walk home."

Track 6 – Station 10: Adjectives and adverbs, Tasks 1 and 2 (Mixed grammar, S. 28)

A police car stops in front of the bank and the police chief jumps out.
"Officer Doyle and I watched all the exits," a police officer tells her quickly, "and nobody left."
The police chief and the two police officers run straight into the bank. They search carefully, but they can't find the bank robber anywhere. The police chief is angry.
"How could the robber escape when you were watching every exit?" she asks the two police officers angrily.
"Well, ma'am," one of the police officers says quietly, "he was very clever and left by the entrance."

Track 7 – Station 4: Past: simple or progressive?, Tasks 1 and 2 (Tenses, S. 35)

The school bell rang. I packed up my things and went into the park. I sat down on a bench. I wanted to wait for the bus there. It was a lovely day. The sun was shining, the birds were singing and boys were playing football. I was tired and fell asleep. When I woke up, I saw that a man was sitting on the bench opposite. He was reading a newspaper. Then I saw that there was a hole in the middle of the newspaper. I noticed that he was watching me. I began to feel nervous. I got up and walked quickly back to the school. When I looked back, I saw that the man was following me. I began to run, but I could still hear his footsteps behind me. They were coming nearer and nearer. And then, at the bus stop, he caught up with me.

Track 8 – Station 1: Comparison of adjectives, Task (Mixed bag, S. 41)

Willy the whale is big. He's very, very big. He's bigger than Olga the orca and Dolly the dolphin. Willy is the biggest animal of the three, but he's slow. He's slower than Olga and Willy. He isn't the slowest animal in the sea, but he's the slowest animal in the group.
Olga the orca is fast. She's faster than Willy and Dolly. She's the fastest animal in the group. Olga is dangerous, too. She's more dangerous than Willy and Dolly. She's the most dangerous of the three.
Dolly the dolphin likes fun and games. She's very playful. She's more playful than Olga and Willy. Dolphins are the most playful animals in the sea. Dolly is clever, too. She can learn new tricks. Dolly is cleverer than most animals. Dolphins are one of the cleverest animals in the sea.
Leo the lion is strong. He's stronger than most animals on land. He's one of the strongest animals in Africa. Don't get too close because he's also very hungry. He's hungrier than he was yesterday. He's the hungriest lion in Africa!
Gary the gorilla has lots of hair. He has hair on his head and his arms and legs. He has hair all over his body. He's a very hairy animal. He's much hairier than a whale or a dolphin. Gary is the hairiest gorilla in the jungle and he doesn't have a comb! Gary can climb trees. He's a good climber. OK, he isn't the best climber in the jungle, but he's a better climber than Leo the lion.
Vera the viper is angry. Vera is always angry, but she's angrier today than she was yesterday. Today she's the angriest animal in the jungle. So be very, very careful because Vera is poisonous. She's more poisonous when she's angry. Today she's very angry and very hungry and she's the most poisonous viper in the jungle!

Track 9 – Station 3: Present and future, Task 1 (Mixed bag, S. 43)

PART 1

Teacher: Please listen carefully. Tomorrow is our class trip. As you already know, we're going to York. We're meeting in front of the school at eight fifteen. Have you all got that?

Pupils: Yes, Mr Wilkinson. We meet at quarter past eight in front of the school.

Teacher: OK. Make a note of the time and the place: eight fifteen in front of the school. The weather forecast for tomorrow isn't good, so bring a raincoat or an umbrella. Girls, we're walking around a lot tomorrow, so wear sensible shoes, OK?

Girls: Yes, Mr Wilkinson.

Teacher: And that goes for the boys, too. Sensible shoes. We're having a picnic lunch tomorrow. The coach driver is stopping somewhere on the way. So bring something to eat and drink. OK?

Pupils: Yes, Mr Wilkinson.

Track 10 – Station 3: Present and future, Task 2 (Mixed bag, S. 43)

PART 2

Teacher: I'm going to read out our timetable for tomorrow. I'd like you all to make a note of the times and the activities. This is important, so listen carefully. We're meeting in front of the school at eight fifteen. Our coach arrives five minutes later at eight twenty. Get on and find a seat as quickly as you can because the coach leaves at exactly eight thirty. I'll repeat that: The coach arrives at eight twenty and it leaves at eight thirty exactly. We won't wait for anyone who is late. At nine o'clock we're stopping for a picnic breakfast. We have about twenty minutes because I want to arrive in York no later than ten fifteen. So write that down: Picnic breakfast at nine o'clock. Arrive in York ten fifteen.
There's a big coach park near York Minster – that's the cathedral. That's where we're going first. There's a guided tour of the cathedral and it starts at ten thirty. The tour takes about an hour. So we can all meet up outside the cathedral at eleven thirty. Have you all made a note of that? Ten thirty – guided tour of cathedral; eleven thirty – meet up again outside. From there we walk to the Jorvik Viking Centre. It's only five minutes or so on foot. You all know where it is. It's also marked on the map of the City Centre that you all have. You can now do what you want and look around by yourselves. This is the main shopping area and there's also a big market. You all have enough money for lunch. There are lots of fish and chip shops, pie shops and there are good things to eat at the market. Be back at the Jorvik Viking Centre by two o'clock. That's when the next tour starts. It takes an hour and a half and then we can look around the Viking Centre shop and café for half an hour and meet outside at four o'clock. OK? So write down: Two o'clock – Jorvik Viking tour starts; four o'clock – meet outside. Then we walk back to our coach. I want to start the journey back at four fifteen, so that we can arrive back in front of the school at six o'clock. That's the time I gave your parents, so we don't want to be late.

Track 11 – Station 8: Present perfect – word order, Task 2 (Mixed bag, S. 48)

Mrs Bradford's washing machine has broken down again. She has already phoned the repair service and they have just called her back. They have promised to send a repairman that afternoon, probably sometime around two o'clock. After the call, Mrs Bradford remembers that she has already made an appointment with her dentist for one o'clock that afternoon. If it takes longer than an hour, she might miss the repairman. And if she's at the dentist's, how will she know if the repairman hasn't already called at her home? But Mrs Bradford has had this problem before and she knows what she has to do. She writes this message and tapes it to her front door:
Dear Repairman,
Please tick the correct statement:
• Yes, I have already called.
• No, I haven't called yet.
Thank you.
Mrs P. Bradford

Bildnachweis:

S. 23: Verkehrszeichen Pfeil
© Nach den amtlichen Vorgaben digital umgesetzt durch: Mediatus, https://commons.wikimedia.org/wiki/File:Zeichen_211_-_Vorgeschriebene_Fahrtrichtung,_hier_rechts,_StVO_2017.svg, Public domain, via Wikimedia Commons

Rauchen verboten
© DrTorstenHenning, https://commons.wikimedia.org/wiki/File:DIN_4844-2_D-P001.svg, Public domain, via Wikimedia Commons

Mitführen von Tieren verboten
© DrTorstenHenning, https://commons.wikimedia.org/wiki/File:DIN_4844-2_D-P014.svg, Public domain, via Wikimedia Commons

No Bikini
© NoBikini.JPG: Cremediaderivative work: Frédéric, https://commons.wikimedia.org/wiki/File:NoBikini.svg, Public domain, via Wikimedia Commons

Campingplatz
© Transportstyrelsen, https://commons.wikimedia.org/wiki/File:Sweden_road_sign_H11.svg, Public domain, via Wikimedia Commons

Jederzeit optimal vorbereitet in den Unterricht?

»Lehrerbüro!

Hier finden Sie alle Unterrichtsmaterialien

der Verlage Auer, AOL-Verlag und PERSEN

immer und überall online verfügbar.

lehrerbuero.de
Jetzt kostenlos testen!

Das **Online-Portal** für Unterricht und Schulalltag!